Helping small businesses prevent substance abuse

Helping small businesses prevent substance abuse

International Labour Office   Geneva

Contents

ANNEXES

Preface

Drug and alcohol abuse is widely prevalent in today's society. It spares no country and no workplace is immune. Well over 50 million people throughout the world are dependent on drugs, and between 12 and 15 per cent of adults are reported to drink at levels hazardous to themselves and to others. In the workplace, substance abuse contributes to accidents, absenteeism, health problems, lowered productivity and job losses.

Substance abuse affects many areas that are of fundamental concern to workers and employers. For workers, substance abuse can lead to injury, disciplinary action and, ultimately, job loss. The welfare of workers' families declines as income is used to purchase alcohol and other drugs. Employers need to consider the safety of their workers, the enterprise and the public, and they also need to take into consideration the increased costs that derive from absenteeism and accidents and result in lower productivity. Governments also need to be mindful of the impact of workplace substance abuse on social welfare systems and on their economies. In today's global economy, where competitiveness, enterprise performance and productivity are of paramount importance, ignoring workplace substance abuse, while absorbing its costs, is not a viable option.

With its tripartite structure, the International Labour Organization (ILO) is in a unique position to have a major impact on workplace substance abuse by linking drug and alcohol prevention to human resources, safety and health, workers' welfare and productivity enhancement programmes. The cornerstone of the ILO's workplace substance abuse programme is the code of practice, *Management of alcohol- and drug-related issues in the workplace*, which was approved by the Governing Body at its 262nd Session in 1995. The code serves as a tool in fulfilling the ILO's mandate by providing the policy and conceptual framework for action in the workplace. A technical cooperation programme embracing technical advisory services, staff training, the launching of programmes and the development of tools and resource materials supplements the ILO's work in this field, with, so far, activities carried out in some 40 countries in all regions.

One of these pilot projects, funded by the Government of Norway, focused specifically on mobilizing small businesses to prevent substance abuse. It was noted that, in the past, it had been mainly the large enterprises that had attempted to implement such programmes, whereas small and medium-sized industries, which employ the largest proportion of the workforce, had taken little action in this area. This was a surprising finding: small enterprises are more vulnerable than larger businesses since substance abuse by even a small percentage of employees can seriously compromise work performance and subsequently affect the productivity of a small business.

The goal of the project was to develop models of successful small enterprise prevention and assistance programmes that could be replicated in similar businesses worldwide. The pilot project was implemented in five countries: Egypt, India, Malaysia, South Africa and Zimbabwe.

This manual is a product of the project and is based on the findings and lessons learned from the experience of the five participating countries and, in particular, on a workplace substance abuse prevention training module developed in South Africa for use by the ILO's Start and Improve Your Business (SIYB) project. It provides background information and a step-by-step guide for developing small business substance abuse prevention initiatives.

The ILO wishes to express its gratitude for the efforts made by all those involved in the work of the project. Special thanks go to the Government of Norway for the funding of the project, to the Director of the Norwegian National Directorate for the Prevention of Alcohol and Drug Problems and to the Secretary-General of the Norwegian Tripartite Committee for the Prevention of Alcohol and Drug Problems in the Workplace (AKAN). The ILO also wishes to recognize the important work of the International Project Coordinator, the national coordinators and the national host organizations as well as the consultants who worked on various aspects of the project and who contributed to developing this manual.

Behrouz Shahandeh
Senior Adviser on Drugs and Alcohol
Programme on Safety, Health and the Environment, SafeWork

Abbreviations

AA   Alcoholics Anonymous

BAC   blood alcohol concentration

EAP   employee assistance programme

ILO   International Labour Organization

NA   Narcotics Anonymous

NGO   non-governmental organization

NPC   National Project Coordinator

PAB   project advisory board

SIYB   Start and Improve Your Business

UNDCP United Nations Drug Control Programme

WHO   World Health Organization

Introduction

Over the past two decades, the abuse of alcohol and drugs has become a major problem for both developing and developed countries. The ever increasing availability of illicit drugs and the aggressive marketing of alcohol have resulted in a growing worldwide consensus that efforts to reduce demand must be increased. This has been reflected in political declarations, resolutions and recommendations adopted by a series of high-level international conferences. Most notable among these are the International Conference on Drug Abuse and Illicit Trafficking (1987); the 17th Special Session of the General Assembly on International Cooperation against Illicit Production, Supply, Demand, Trafficking and Distribution of Narcotics and Psychotropic Substances (1998); and the World Ministerial Summit to Reduce the Demand for Drugs and to Combat the Cocaine Threat (1990).

The ILO concerns itself with all issues that have an impact on the world of work. Substance abuse is now a matter of great importance to all its tripartite members: governments, employers' and workers' organizations. At the government level, substance abuse is becoming a major social, legal and economic issue. At the enterprise level, its repercussions include accidents, absenteeism and lost productivity. At the worker level, it can lead to impaired health, deteriorating work relationships, job losses as well as family, legal and economic problems.

Increasingly, large employers understand that the health and safety of their workers affect the health of their businesses, and that substance abuse is part of the picture. They realize that if there is substance abuse in their community, it is likely to be a problem in their workforce. There is also growing recognition that, at times, the workplace itself can contribute to substance abuse through conditions such as stress and company attitudes towards alcohol or other drug use. Many large businesses now recognize that the employer, particularly when supported by the workers, is in a strong position to prevent or reduce workplace drug or alcohol problems, and that it is good business to do so.

Most people, however, work in small businesses, and the small business sector has been slower to take action on substance abuse. Some owners/managers do not feel that it is the role of business to address "social problems". Others don't see substance abuse as a problem for their businesses. Yet others acknowledge it to be a problem and may feel some sense of responsibility towards their workers, but do not believe they have the time, money or knowledge to deal with the issue.

There is good reason, however, for the small business sector to pay more attention to substance abuse and related health problems. Even minor inefficiencies caused by substance abuse can have a detrimental effect on the competitiveness of a small firm, which depends so much on the contribution of each worker, while an accident causing serious injury or death could have devastating consequences for a small business. The demanding conditions associated with work in small firms can place everyone – managers and workers – at higher risk from substance abuse. Moreover, with large companies paying more attention to this issue, small companies may become the preferred place of employment for substance-abusing workers. Consequently, substance abuse has become a "bottom-line" issue for small enterprises.

A number of ILO meetings have highlighted the need to focus on the small business sector and to assist this large segment of the working population in substance abuse prevention. These include the ILO/United States Tripartite Symposium on Drug and Alcohol

Prevention and Assistance Programmes in the Workplace (1991)[1] and the Seminar on International Information Exchange on Drugs and Alcohol in the Workplace (1991).[2] Substance abuse prevention for small businesses has also been a common recommendation of ILO-executed projects in many countries, including Chile, India, Jamaica, Mauritius, Philippines, Sri Lanka, Thailand and Zimbabwe.

The ILO pilot project

Over the years, the ILO has developed a wealth of knowledge and experience in the realm of substance abuse prevention programming and small businesses in developing countries. In particular, the ILO's SIYB programme has gained considerable expertise in working with small businesses. Building on this experience, the ILO developed and implemented a pilot project to assist small businesses in addressing the substance abuse problem in their workplaces. Entitled *Mobilizing Small Businesses to Prevent Substance Abuse* (INT/95/M27/NOR), the pilot project was interregional and operated at the national level in five countries in Africa and Asia: Egypt, India, Malaysia, South Africa and Zimbabwe.

The pilot project ran from July 1996 to March 2000 and was exploratory in nature. Its long-term objective was the prevention and reduction of substance abuse and the improved health, safety and welfare of workers and their families. In the short term, that is, by the end of the project, it was hoped that: the necessary administrative, technical and resource capabilities would be established in each participating country; a general model on drug abuse prevention in small businesses would have been adopted to support the small business community in developing similar programmes worldwide; and drug prevention strategies and programmes would become integrated into the other management practices of the participating enterprises.

The project was divided into three phases:

- **A preparatory phase** (to be completed in the project's first year): This included the creation of the project's implementation infrastructure and the establishment of a Tripartite Advisory Board. The phase entailed a review of the relevant ongoing experiences in each participating country, the conceptualization of the pilot small business prevention models, the identification and mobilization of community financial resources and the identification of the most effective channels for reaching and mobilizing small businesses to participate in the project. In addition, it addressed the hiring of project staff, the preparation of awareness and training materials as well as the development of an action plan for the entire course of the project, a workplan for the first year and a media campaign.

- **The implementation phase** (to start at the beginning of the second year and to be completed by the end of the project): This included the kick-off of the media campaign, the recruitment of small businesses, the adaptation of the project models to the needs of the participating small businesses and the running of specialized orientation seminars, awareness activities and training sessions.

- **The evaluation phase** (to be continuous and to run parallel with the other project activities): This phase focused on sharing experiences with other communities and countries including any adaptations and mechanisms developed to ensure that the prevention initiatives were sustained.

---

[1] Sponsored by the United States Department of Labor.
[2] Jointly sponsored by the ILO, the United States National Institute on Drug Abuse and the Government of Norway.

This manual draws upon the findings of the ILO pilot project. Its target audiences are the host organizations that sponsor, fund and provide overall direction to the projects and the project managers who are responsible for implementing them. The guidelines in this manual are not prescriptive but are meant to be adapted to fit the political, social, cultural and financial environments of each new initiative.

The ILO code of practice

The ILO has found that substance abuse prevention programmes in the workplace tend to be more effective when they have been developed within a policy framework that clearly defines roles and responsibilities, specifies the scope of activities and explains the kind of assistance that is available. In addition, these programmes are easier to implement and more acceptable to workers if they have been formulated through joint labour – management consultations and agreements. And, of course, they must be developed within the context of national legislation and country culture.

It was against this background that the ILO developed the code of practice, *Management of alcohol- and drug-related issues in the workplace*, published in 1996. The objective of the code is to promote the prevention, reduction and management of alcohol- and other drug-related problems in the workplace. It is the framework within which the ILO recommends that governments and employers' and workers' organizations develop and implement workplace substance abuse prevention programmes.

The key points of the code of practice are as follows:

1. Alcohol and drug policies and programmes should promote the prevention, reduction and management of alcohol- and drug-related problems in the workplace. This code applies to all types of public and private employment, including the informal sector. Legislation and national policy should be determined after consultations with the representatives of the employers' and workers' organizations.

2. Alcohol and drug problems should be considered as health problems and therefore should be dealt with in the same way as any other health problem at work, without any discrimination, and covered by the health-care systems (public or private) as appropriate.

3. Employers and workers and their representatives should jointly assess the effects of alcohol and drug use in the workplace and should cooperate in developing a written policy for the enterprise.

4. Employers, in cooperation with workers and their representatives, should do what is reasonably practicable to identify job situations that contribute to alcohol- and drug-related problems and take appropriate preventive or remedial action.

5. The same restrictions or prohibitions with respect to alcohol and drugs should apply to both management personnel and workers, so that there is a clear and unambiguous policy.

6. Information, education and training programmes concerning alcohol and drugs should be undertaken to promote health and safety in the workplace and should be integrated where feasible into broad-based health programmes.

7. Employers should establish a system to ensure the confidentiality of all information communicated to them concerning alcohol- and drug-related problems. Workers should be informed of exceptions to confidentiality arising from legal, professional or ethical principles.

8. Testing of bodily samples for alcohol and drugs in the context of employment involves moral, ethical and legal issues of fundamental importance, requiring a determination of when it is fair and appropriate to conduct such testing.

9. The stability that ensues from holding a job is frequently an important factor in facilitating recovery from alcohol- and drug-related problems. Therefore, the social partners should acknowledge the special role the workplace may play in assisting individuals with such problems.

10. Workers who seek treatment and rehabilitation for alcohol- or drug-related problems should not be discriminated against by the employer and should enjoy normal job security and the same opportunities for transfer and advancement as their colleagues.

11. It should be recognized that the employer has the authority to discipline workers for employment-related misconduct associated with alcohol and drugs. However, counselling, treatment and rehabilitation should be the preferred course of action. Should a worker fail to cooperate fully with the treatment programme, the employer may take disciplinary action as considered appropriate.

12. The employer should adopt the principle of non-discrimination in employment based on previous or current use of alcohol or drugs in accordance with national law and regulations.

The code is a guide for establishing workplace substance abuse prevention programmes and is not intended to replace or override any international standard or national law or regulation that might be more protective. The implementation of any provision of the code must also take into consideration the particular cultural, legal, social, political and economic circumstances of each country and any collective agreements already in existence.

PART I
Substance abuse prevention: The big picture

1. Substance abuse

The use of psychoactive substances for their mood changing effects is not a new phenomenon, and in certain traditions, they have been part of religious events and celebrations. When they are abused, it is usually due to a combination of personal, inter-personal, environmental or genetic factors. In some cases, substance abuse can result in psychological and physical dependence.

The use and abuse of psychoactive substances are not restricted to any specific group, country, culture or ideology, although the substances used have varied by geographic area and availability. With globalization, however, alcohol and a wide range of drugs are becoming more readily accessible and more frequently used. The use of unfamiliar psychoactive substances, sometimes in combination with other substances, which may also be psychoactive, can increase the rate of dependency and the harmful effects on the mind and body.

1.1. Substances of abuse

Alcohol, which includes beer, wine and spirits and the pure alcohol present in non-prescription medications, and illegal drugs (cannabis, heroin, methamfetamine, cocaine and crack, hallucinogens and amfetamine-type stimulants) are the two groups of substance abuse.

Alcohol

Ethanol is the active ingredient that is present in every type of alcoholic beverage. The harmful effects of alcohol consumption can include drowsiness, slower reaction times, deterioration of motor performance and coordination skills, loss of concentration and memory, and deterioration in intellectual performance. Long-term use of alcohol can cause cirrhosis. Alcohol poisoning and death can occur if alcohol is consumed in excess, either in a single instance or over an extended period of time.

What is considered an acceptable level of consumption varies from country to country and from culture to culture. Per capita consumption of alcohol in a given society is the strongest predictor of the number and types of problems related to substance abuse that will occur in that society and subsequently in the workplace. A doubling of the per capita consumption could indicate a three- to four-fold increase in the number of individuals who are drinking at levels dangerous to themselves and others. More information on alcohol can be found in Annex I.

Illegal drugs [1]

In general, drugs can be divided into three categories according to their pharmacological effects:

- depressants, such as heroin, morphine and opium;

- stimulants, such as amfetamines, cocaine and crack; and

- hallucinogens, such as cannabis, LSD (lysergic acid diethylamide or "acid") and MDMA (methylenedioxymethamfetamine or "ecstasy"), which also has stimulating effects.

The effects of drugs on the central nervous system vary enormously and can range from increased alertness, restlessness, irritability and anxiety to depression, dizziness, sleeplessness, bizarre and sometimes violent behaviour and distorted perceptions of depth, time, size and shape of objects and movement. For more information on specific drugs of abuse, see Annex II.

Medications and inhalants

The ILO pilot project did not include medications and inhalants since relatively little is known about the extent to which they are used in the workplace. Nevertheless, since certain categories of medications and inhalants have significant side effects, which could have a detrimental effect on work performance, employers and workers need to be aware of their potential for abuse. Non-prescription medications (such as sleeping aids, cold and cough medicines and antihistamines), prescription medications (such as tranquillizers, anti-depressants, pain killers, notably morphine and codeine, and muscle relaxants) and inhalants (glue, solvents and paints) all have side effects.

1.2. Physiological effects

The way people react to alcohol and drugs can vary greatly. Body size, gender and genetics all play a part. Important independent factors include:

- the amount consumed at one time;

- past experience;

- the mood and activity of the user;

- the time and place of consumption;

- the presence of other people;

- the simultaneous use of other substances of abuse; and

- the physical and mental health of the user.

When it comes to body size, the larger a person is, the smaller the effect alcohol will have on that person. This is because a heavier person has more blood and water in which to dilute alcohol.

---

[1] Some drugs, which are illegal in one country, may be considered less harmful, or even legal, in another. Some can be illegal except when used in religious or cultural contexts. Some psychoactive substances may be local in production and use and not regulated at all. Drugs such as LSD and MDMA are produced synthetically. N.B. The spelling of drugs in this publication follow the 92/27/EEC directive, which requires the use of the Recommended International Non-proprietary Name (rINN). For example, amphetamine becomes amfetamine.

Women generally tolerate alcohol less well than men, even those with the same body weight. Women have a higher percentage of body fat and a lower percentage of body water than men. Adipose (fat tissues) is not easily penetrated by alcohol, which means there will be a higher concentration of alcohol in the bloodstream. Women also have fewer of the enzymes that metabolize alcohol in the stomach wall, so that most of the alcohol absorption in women takes place in the small intestine, which leads to a rapid increase in blood alcohol concentration (BAC) levels. Thus, a woman drinking the same amount of alcohol as a man of identical weight will develop a higher BAC level. The contact time between the alcohol consumed and the various organs of the body will also be longer, which puts women at greater risk from all types of alcohol-related conditions.

Finally, the absence of or damage to certain genes may increase the likelihood of a person developing a dependency.

1.3. Socio-demographic factors

Substance use and abuse are not evenly distributed throughout any given population. Studies have shown that adolescents tend to drink alcohol sporadically during the week, reaching peaks at weekends, while the consumption pattern of men between the ages of 35 and 50 is more evenly spread over weekdays, with no high peaks. People over the age of 50 tend to limit their drinking. For women, the patterns are similar, although, on average, they consume much lower levels of alcohol than men.

Young people are the main users of drugs. In the United Kingdom and the United States, large numbers of young people admit to having used drugs at least once. In some continental European countries, the percentage of young people reporting drug use is lower, although still considerable. Many countries, though, do not have any reliable data on drug use.

1.4. Addressing substance abuse

Substance abuse is a sensitive issue and dealing with it is no easy matter. Abusers can be extremely defensive when approached about their alcohol or drug use, and often resort to a variety of techniques, including denial, rationalization, minimization and selective recall, to manipulate family, friends, co-workers and supervisors. In addition, the signs and symptoms of substance abuse are frequently characteristics of other medical conditions. Therefore, any type of assessment, counselling or referral based on the issue of substance abuse should be done by a health-care professional with specialist training in the field.

As with all medical conditions, prevention is much more effective and much less costly than treating the full-blown condition. Prevention can be defined as a proactive process that empowers individuals to meet the challenges of events and transitions in their lives by developing and reinforcing the skills that will help them to cope.

2. The paradigm shift to prevention

Traditionally, the focus of workplace substance abuse programmes has been on providing treatment and rehabilitation to dependent workers. However, since most workers are not, in fact, dependent on alcohol or drugs (in some countries, it is estimated that only ten in 100 people have an alcohol or drug problem and, of those ten, only three have become dependent), valuable resources have often been concentrated on too few workers, too late. However, by making prevention rather than intervention in the workplace the focus, the entire workforce are included, which should lead to fewer workers developing substance abuse problems.

There are three main reasons why it makes sense to implement a substance abuse prevention programme in the workplace:

- Prevention initiatives emphasize worker health, well-being and safety, which in turn increase enterprise productivity and competitiveness. This positive approach removes the stigma of substance abuse from the workplace. Both management and labour can support initiatives to employers, workers' representatives and workers in a non-threatening manner.

- A prevention programme aimed at all workers benefits the entire enterprise and is less expensive than intervention and treatment. Epidemiological studies have shown that the incidence of alcohol- or drug-related problems is correlated to consumption (the greater the consumption, the greater the number of incidents such as accidents, absenteeism, violence and harassment).

- Alcohol and drugs can potentially interact with other chemical substances in the workplace, leading to side effects such as dizziness, drowsiness and loss of concentration.

2.1. The traffic light analogy

Using the analogy of a traffic light, the level of a worker's use of alcohol or drugs can be divided into one of three zones: the green zone, the amber zone or the red zone.

- Green zone: Workers who don't drink any alcohol or drink only in moderation and those who never use illegal drugs fall within the green zone. Their intake of alcohol takes into account the demands of the setting in which consumption takes place or in which they will be immediately after consumption (for example, traffic rules, work requirements). These workers can safely continue their drinking patterns – they have a green light.

- Amber zone: Workers in this zone use alcohol to excess or use drugs but are not yet dependent on these substances. Therefore, they are generally able to change their habits themselves or with the help of professional counsellors. Workers in this zone need to exercise caution in their use of alcohol and drugs. They need to cut down, or in some cases stop, their intake of alcohol and, in the case of drugs, stop using them altogether. These workers have an amber light.

- Red zone: Red means stop. Workers in the red zone are dependent on one or more psychoactive substances. They experience serious problems at work and in other areas of their lives. Workers in this zone usually need professional help or treatment to help them return to normal, at work and in private.

Figure 2.1. The traffic light as metaphor

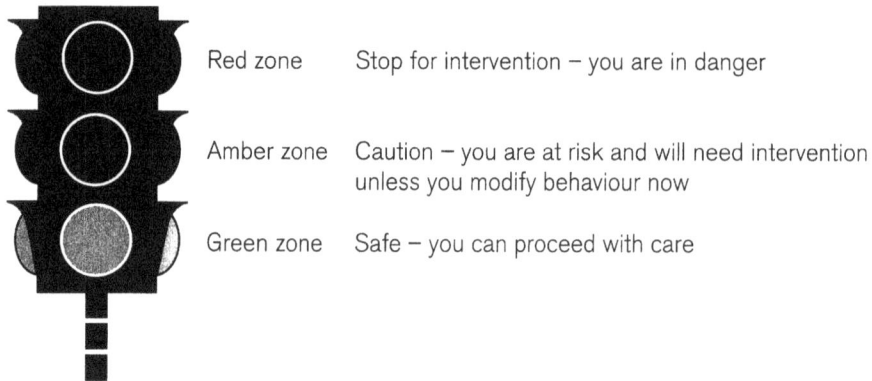

Red zone — Stop for intervention – you are in danger

Amber zone — Caution – you are at risk and will need intervention unless you modify behaviour now

Green zone — Safe – you can proceed with care

Moving from the green zone to the red zone is a process that can take from only a few months, especially in the case of certain drugs, to up to several years. The progression from one zone to the next is not usually marked by a single event or by a specific amount of the substance consumed. In moving from green to amber, moderate use gradually develops into problem use. As substance abuse increases, the individual moves through the amber zone and may eventually become dependent. Because there is no uniquely identifiable event, only health professionals trained in substance abuse can determine when an individual becomes dependent.

Traditional workplace substance abuse programmes focus almost exclusively on providing assistance to workers in the red zone. As a result, resources are concentrated on a small number of workers who are difficult to treat.

Figure 2.2. The traditional approach

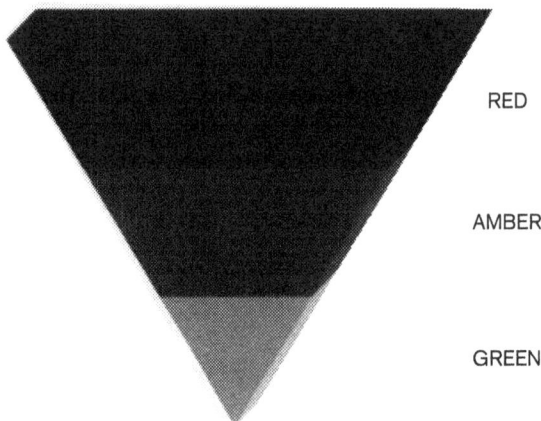

Figure 2.3. The prevention approach

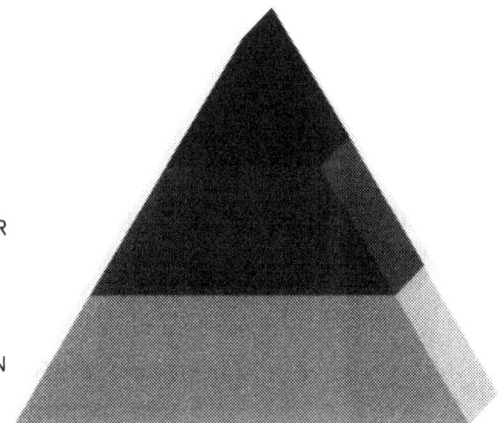

RED

AMBER

GREEN

By shifting to a substance abuse **prevention** programme, the focus expands to the entire workforce, although the emphasis is on workers in the green and amber zones. Prevention programmes now concentrate their resources on these workers, although they still provide help for workers in the red zone.

Moderate versus heavy drinkers

Although chronic alcohol consumption can have a dramatic economic and social influence on the workplace, the negative effect of moderate alcohol consumption should not be underestimated.

Laboratory studies indicate that the amount of alcohol in even a single commercial cocktail can affect the way a person functions and interacts. Recent evidence also suggests that intermittent heavy alcohol use by moderate consumers can result in changes in performance even after BAC levels have returned to zero. As moderate users of alcohol occasionally drink to excess and subsequently become involved in alcohol-related incidents, their behaviour can have a detrimental effect on workplace safety and performance.

Since workers in the green and amber zones far outnumber heavy or dependent drinkers, the total number of alcohol-related incidents caused by moderate drinkers may be greater than total number of incidents caused by heavy or dependent drinkers. Therefore, it follows that a substance abuse programme that focuses on prevention and early intervention may have a greater impact on health and safety and on enterprise productivity than one that deals only with workers in the red zone.

2.2. Promoting good health

An important strategy of substance abuse prevention programmes is to encourage people to avoid abusing substances in the first place and to maintain a healthy lifestyle. Since the very experience of being in good health can reinforce a person's motivation to maintain such a lifestyle, good health is a powerful tool in learning to avoid substance abuse.

In the past few years, preventing the spread of HIV/AIDS has become a particularly urgent aspect of health promotion. The risk of infection is closely linked to alcohol and drug abuse since people under the influence of these substances are more likely to have unprotected sex. Drug users who inject their drugs are particularly at risk of infection as sharing needles can transfer the virus. The relationship between substance abuse, sexual behaviour and the risk of HIV should be stressed at every possible occasion.[1]

2.3. The role of management

When the focus on dealing with substance abuse moves from treatment to prevention, responsibility shifts from the health and medical community to managers in the workplace. However, although policy decisions concerning the scope and operation of the prevention programme rest with management, senior managers should work together with workers' representatives on formulating policies on the following issues:

- the use of alcohol and drugs (including prescription drugs) before and during working hours;
- the availability of alcohol at the worksite;
- the scope and content of awareness campaigns;
- the training of supervisors;
- the education of workers;
- the degree to which families will be covered;
- circumstances triggering offers of treatment and rehabilitation; and
- the financial commitment of the company in supporting treatment and rehabilitation.

[1] Additional information on HIV/AIDS policy and programme development, including the ILO code of practice, *HIV/AIDS and the world of work*, can be found on the ILO website at: http://www.ilo.org/public/english/protection/safework/cops/english/download/e000008.pdf

2.4. Links with the community and the family

Small businesses are an important aspect of national economies and are deeply intertwined in the lives of local communities, which they often serve and from which they draw their workforce. Therefore, the use and abuse of alcohol and drugs in the small business workplace cannot be considered without referring to the community and the family.

Individuals develop their beliefs and values in the context of social norms and official regulations and in close interplay with family and friends. They, their families and the local community form a social network that includes the company. Consequently, it is not surprising that the degree of tolerance in a community influences the availability of dependency-creating substances and their acceptance in the workplace. Conversely, a permissive attitude towards substance abuse in the workplace has a strong influence on workers' use of alcohol and drugs in their free time.

Problems related to alcohol and drugs can arise as a consequence of personal, family or social circumstances, or they can be connected to certain working conditions. In most cases, they probably result from a combination of these factors. Whatever the causes, substance abuse has an adverse effect on the health and well-being of workers and on the competitiveness of enterprises. It also has a negative impact on the private lives of individuals, especially on their relationships with their family and friends.

The welfare of families can suffer greatly when the main earner of a family has a substance abuse problem. Conversely, the personal problems of workers and their families may cause or increase substance abuse, which subsequently has an impact on the workplace. Therefore, it would make sense to include family members in workplace substance abuse prevention programmes.

In most societies, the structure of the family has been changing dramatically over the past few decades. With rising numbers of single parents, more people living alone and economic migration, the influence and support of the traditional family and social networks are weakened. A clear distinction between work and home cannot be made in all jobs. In the maritime sector or the transport industry, for example, workers spend long periods away from home. Many industries and services require their employees to do night shifts and work irregular hours. This affects family life, and the way that families react is crucial to the well-being of workers.

Young workers are particularly vulnerable when it comes to substance abuse. Because of their youth, they are more likely to experiment with alcohol and drugs. They are also more vulnerable to peer pressure and to the effects of different substances but lack the experience to deal with them. Therefore, finding out about their attitudes and behaviour through workplace substance prevention programmes makes good sense. Early investment in education is also critical, and can be done most effectively when enterprises, schools, health-care and community organizations and the public sector work together.

A substance abuse prevention programme must take into account changes in the world of work, the interaction between work and family, the availability of alcohol and drugs and cultural and sub-cultural norms that support substance use. The ultimate objective is to promote a positive, sustainable workplace culture and a healthy workforce.

Family and community initiatives can play a key role in substance abuse prevention programmes. They can include:

- organizing school-based activities during and after school hours;
- creating awareness materials for parents and children;
- running training and employment initiatives for recovering workers;
- lobbying within the community to establish regulations that support substance abuse prevention programmes and related services; and
- providing community recreation facilities and activities.

Another way in which the community can work with local enterprises is in the treatment and rehabilitation of drug-dependent workers. A community may have costly treatment facilities without having given due consideration to vocational training or rehabilitation programmes, even though the evidence suggests that employment during and after treatment contributes significantly to the long-term recovery of dependent workers. Employers could, therefore, play a vital role by integrating employment opportunities into alcohol and drug treatment programmes.

3. Substance abuse and the workplace

Along with stress, fatigue and illness, alcohol and drug abuse can cause serious workplace impairment. It occurs in many workplaces and at all levels, from top management to rank-and-file workers.

The telltale signs of a worker with a substance abuse problem include:

- **Deterioration in performance:** inconsistent work quality, deteriorating productivity, an erratic work pace, poorer levels of concentration, signs of fatigue, an increase in mistakes, carelessness and errors in judgement.

- **An increase in absenteeism and poor attendance:** tardiness in arriving for work or absent more frequently (especially before and after weekends and holidays), more frequent absences from work station, extended lunch hours and breaks, and leaving early at the end of the working day.

- **Changes in attitude and physical appearance:** shifting the blame to others, neglecting details, sloppy work habits, avoiding co-workers and supervisors, deteriorating work relationships and deteriorating appearance and hygiene.

- **An increase in health and safety hazards:** more worksite accidents and damaged or destroyed machinery, needless risk-taking and disregard for the safety of co-workers.

- **The emergence of domestic problems:** financial and family problems.

3.1. Post-use impairment

The harm done in the workplace by substance abusers is due not only to the immediate effects of drugs and alcohol but also to post-use impairment, a condition commonly referred to as the "hangover effect". Post-use impairment can have an adverse effect on the following functions of a worker:

- reaction time (responses are slower);
- motor performance (clumsy movements and poor coordination);
- sight (blurred vision);
- mood (aggression or depression);
- learning and memory (loss of concentration); and
- intellectual performance (impairment of logical thinking).

The hangover effect impairs workers' ability to cope with high-risk situations and makes them more likely to endanger their co-workers and themselves. The abuse of alcohol and drugs in some occupations, particularly in the transportation sector, can also put the general public at risk. In a study[1] to demonstrate the hangover effect, airline pilots were asked to perform routine tasks in a flight simulator under three alcohol test conditions. The results were as follows:

---

[1] J. G. Modell and J. M. Mountz, "Drinking and flying: The problem of alcohol use by pilots", in *New England Journal of Medicine*, Vol. 323, No. 7, 1990, pp. 455-461.

- First test: Before the consumption of any alcohol, only 10 per cent of the pilots could not perform all the set tasks correctly.
- Second test: After reaching a BAC level of 0.10/100ml, 89 per cent of the pilots could not perform all the tasks correctly.
- Third test: Fourteen hours later, after all the alcohol had left their systems, 68 per cent of the pilots could still not perform all the tasks correctly.

3.2. The costs of substance abuse

Substance abuse can have a profound effect on businesses of all sizes, on family members and on the community at large. Besides the concern it raises on a personal level, when any worker abuses alcohol or drugs to the extent that it affects workplace performance, the consequences, reflected in the following areas, can be numerous and costly.

Productivity

- Poor work needing to be redone, resulting in a waste of materials
- Lateness and absenteeism
- Co-workers covering for the substance-abusing worker
- Loss of skills when a worker leaves the enterprise due to injury or job termination
- Replacement costs, including recruitment and orientation

Legal issues

- The need to show that sufficient action to protect worker health and safety was taken in the event of an accident
- Human rights challenges if a dependent worker is not dealt with fairly
- Labour law violations if workers are not disciplined in a just manner
- Increase in theft and fraud

Working environment and conditions

- Declining work relationships
- Damage to worker morale
- Additional stress to the owner/manager

Health and safety

- Deteriorating health of workers
- Accidents resulting in injury or death to the worker, co-workers or the public
- Deteriorating relationships with family and friends
- Loss of job and career prospects

Community concerns

- Increasing unemployment and welfare costs
- Loss of jobs and a drop in tax revenues

3.3. Working conditions

Certain working conditions can place owners/managers and workers at greater risk from health problems, including substance abuse. Studies have shown the following to be of particular concern:

- excessive stress and fatigue;
- boredom due to repetitive work;
- unrealistic expectations of the owner/manager or other workers;
- lack of supervision;
- job insecurity;
- shift and night work;
- poor communication;
- unclear roles and responsibilities; and
- little or no control over work.

3.4. The leverage of the workplace

Whether substance abuse is brought into the workplace by a worker or whether it is linked to certain workplace conditions, businesses of all sizes can play an important role in educating their employees about alcohol and drug abuse as well as in identifying workers with problems. Indeed, since substance abusers are more likely to take action when faced with the possibility of losing their job than almost any other outcome, including the loss of family and friends, the workplace is one of the most effective agents of change in patterns of substance abuse.

- The entire working population, from adolescents to mature adults, can be reached through workplace programmes.
- There are workers at risk from developing substance abuse in all workplaces.
- In the workplace, the target group for substance abuse prevention is a captive audience.
- Employment is one of the most reliable supports for coping successfully with problems of abuse.
- The greatest potential for reducing alcohol- and drug-related injury is outside the context of hospitals and clinics.

PART II
The small business connection

4. Defining a small business

The definition of what constitutes a small business varies from country to country. Generally, though, a small business is a business where either employee numbers are small or where the principal decision-making functions rest with the owner. In most cases, however, a small business is categorized by employee number. In countries where the largest businesses employ around 100 workers, "small" can mean ten or fewer workers. In other countries, where large businesses employ from between 10,000 to 50,000 workers or more, "small" can mean as many as 500 workers. It may also be helpful to think of defining a small business in terms of a range in worker numbers (for example, from five to 25, five to 50, five to 100), bearing in mind that the larger the number of workers, the more sophisticated a preventive substance abuse programme can be.

In today's fast-changing social and economic environment, small firms are facing new competitive requirements that call for a highly competent and committed workforce. As a result, there has been a huge increase in the interest shown to supporting and promoting small businesses and their workers to help them meet these new competitive needs. Companies that are unable to meet today's high production and service standards are likely to fail. This increase in competitiveness arising from the globalization of economies can place added pressure on owners/managers and their workers.

In this context, the impact of substance abuse on small businesses is becoming of greater concern to governments, to the small business community and to workers in small enterprises. The reasons for this concern include:

- the move from large corporations and companies to smaller, more adaptable and more manageable units;
- the expansion of the small (and medium) business sector worldwide;
- the employment of up to 80 per cent of workers worldwide in small businesses;
- the fact that approximately 80 per cent of new jobs are created in this sector; and,
- the adaptability of small businesses to meet changing market demands.

Small businesses are seen as increasingly important "engines" to many economies, particularly in developing countries. Since key decisions rest mainly with the owner/manager, small enterprises are in a position to be innovative and to respond quickly to market opportunities at a pace that larger enterprises often find difficult to match. There appears to be limitless opportunities in the global marketplace for small businesses that are adaptable, innovative, produce high-quality products and have high levels of productivity.

Running a small business can be daunting, however. Most small business owners/managers operate in survival mode. Lack of time and little money, combined with a desire for independence and flexibility, create a management style that is informal and reactive. Also, many small businesses often employ family and friends, which creates a company atmosphere that is more personal than in larger enterprises.

Small businesses differ significantly from large corporations; they are not simply smaller versions of large businesses. So what works in a large business cannot just be reduced to meet the needs of a small business. The following are common characteristics of most small businesses that set them clearly apart from larger companies:

- Owners/managers work on-site with workers.
- The small number of workers means that the owner/manager directs all the work and makes all the decisions.
- Because owners/managers are closely involved in their businesses, their attitudes and actions determine the working culture, making small businesses as different as the individuals who own them.
- The smallest businesses are often either exempt from national labour laws or operate in the informal sector.
- Owners/managers are resistant to government bureaucracy and paperwork.
- Owners/managers value autonomy and independence.
- The lack of documented operating procedures to respond to changing needs or problems results in "seat of the pants" management.
- The lack of planning and management skills means that owners/managers often practise crisis management.
- Few resources exist for employee training or development.
- Workers have little or no involvement with formal labour organizations.
- Small businesses rely heavily on repeat customers, so quality products and services are essential.
- Higher accident rates and more frequent employee turnover are common.
- Owners/managers are reluctant to seek advice and assistance from outsiders and, regardless of the nature of the problem, are more likely to consult with the owners/managers of other small businesses than with experts.
- Small business owners/managers are less likely to be networked at the national level and harder to access through established communications channels.

5. Substance abuse prevention and small businesses

Many large businesses have comprehensive programmes to address the issue of substance abuse. However, due to their very nature, most small businesses cannot, and indeed should not, be expected to establish comparable programmes. Rather, it makes more sense for small businesses to tackle substance abuse prevention through initiatives that meet their particular needs.

Small businesses vary tremendously in financial status, type of workforce and occupational health and safety concerns. However, they do share some general characteristics that can increase the frequency and affect the nature of substance abuse problems:

- Owners/managers often drive themselves and their workers too hard, putting themselves under a lot of stress, which can lead to substance abuse.

- Small enterprises tend to hire younger, less experienced workers who, in most societies, are the biggest consumers of alcohol and drugs.

- Increasingly, large firms are developing strict policies on substance abuse, so substance abusers seek employment in smaller firms where less attention is paid to this issue.

- With fewer workers in a small firm, the problems caused by a substance-abusing worker will have a relatively greater impact.

- Were a substance-abusing worker in a safety-sensitive position to cause injury or death to a co-worker or customer, a small company (with fewer resources to deal with the resulting legal issues and bad publicity) could go out of business.

- Some small firms are often involved in highly sensitive commercial activities (for example, financial or security services) and may lack the resources to deal with the consequences of this work being mishandled.

Recognizing the barriers to developing effective substance abuse prevention initiatives is important when supporting small business action on substance abuse. For the most part, the business owners/managers who participated in the ILO pilot project, *Mobilizing Small Businesses to Prevent Substance Abuse*, corroborated the following:

- They had little awareness of the impact substance abuse could have on their businesses (for example, bottom-line issues).

- They had very little understanding of the dynamics of substance abuse.

- They did not necessarily recognize that they had a role to play in substance abuse prevention, which could benefit both their workers and themselves.

- They tended either to ignore the problem or use punitive methods when dealing with workers with substance abuse-related problems (for example, terminating jobs).

- Since they did not have even the most rudimentary management systems in place and did not have policies on other operations or processes, they did not see the need to have a policy on substance abuse.

- They feared reprisals from their workforce, family and friends.

- They feared dealing with a potentially explosive subject without having any knowledge or skill in the area.

- They preferred more informal ways of running their businesses, relying on relationships rather than rules. When this doesn't work, it is easier to fire a worker, regardless of legislation or relationship.

However, once the owners/managers had acquired some basic knowledge and insight about substance abuse and its effects on the workplace, they were much more willing to raise awareness, educate their workers and allow workers to seek help.

Conversely, it is important to recognize the advantages of working with small businesses:

- It is often easier for owners/managers to make rapid changes to work practices, since they make all the decisions anyway.

- Because of the size and informality of the workplace, simple and inexpensive measures can be effective.

- Small business owners/managers can draw support and resources from community substance abuse prevention programmes.

- Owners/managers are more likely to feel responsible for their workers and to be more solicitous about their welfare.

- Owners/managers are action-oriented and want practical options rather than conceptual approaches.

The number of small businesses with substance abuse problems is growing worldwide. Since this is an issue that leaves many owners/managers overwhelmed, it is an area in which they are in urgent need of assistance.

PART III
Establishing a substance abuse prevention programme

6. The impact of pre-existing legislative and cultural norms

This third and final section is aimed primarily, though not exclusively, at the project manager, who shoulders the greatest responsibility when it comes to implementing a substance abuse prevention programme for small businesses. The word "project" is used throughout Part III to refer to the substance abuse prevention programme, which you, as project manager, will help your local small business community put into effect.

Certain attitudes and institutions need to be in place before a substance abuse prevention programme can be got off the ground. There are four key elements that constitute the very basis of the project and their existence is a prerequisite for its success. However, they are outside the project's control, and if even one of these elements is absent, the prospects for the project's long-term success are seriously diminished.

6.1. National legislation and a culture that support restrictions on the use of alcohol and drugs

The culture of the locality in which the project is to be implemented must recognize the need to place restrictions on the use of alcohol and drugs for the health and safety of its citizens. The existence of national or local legislation to restrict the use of alcohol and drugs in specific circumstances will make it much easier for you, as the project manager, and the project advisory board (PAB) to convince small business owners/managers of the necessity of such restrictions in the workplace.

Laws and regulations: Your project should comply with the relevant laws and regulations. Active enforcement of your country's existing substance abuse-related legislation lends legitimacy to your project's goals.

Since small business owners/managers are often unaware of government regulations, you need to be conversant with them, including the following:

- worker health and safety;
- human rights concerning workers, dependencies and disabilities;
- labour laws pertaining to the dismissal of workers;
- laws concerning the sale and use of alcohol; and
- laws concerning the possession and trafficking of illicit drugs.

Culture and community: Your project needs to reflect the values and attitudes of the culture and the community. It is important that businesses know that the aim of the project is not to interfere with the social norms but to reduce and prevent workplace accidents, injuries and other alcohol- and drug-related problems.

6.2. Understanding dependency as a health problem

Acknowledging the fact that alcohol and drug dependency is a health problem that can be treated and not a moral weakness is important to the acceptance of the programme. When dependency is seen as a progressive, treatable health problem, the advantage of a prevention programme and the need for professional treatment will make much more sense to small business owners/managers and workers, and they will also see the programme as less threatening.

Where dependency is not viewed as a health problem, the reaction of business owners/managers to workers who abuse alcohol or drugs is often very harsh, frequently resulting in job termination. This approach, however, only transfers the problem to another employer or to the community at large.

6.3. The existence and effectiveness of community support services

Because of limited internal resources, most small business owners/managers need to turn to community support organizations to obtain inexpensive or free outside expertise and assistance for substance abuse prevention programming. Community support services can provide substance abuse awareness materials, training for small business owners/managers and workers, and assistance in developing a workplace policy and in responding to alcohol- or drug-related emergencies. These services should include individuals or groups who have experience in working with small businesses, so that they speak the language of small business, have credibility with and access to the small business community and can provide practical advice and assistance.

Before selecting community services to support the project, you must make site visits or have extensive contacts to ensure that they can provide the specialized expertise your project needs. You have to be very clear about these services when you speak with the different organizations, so that there are no misunderstandings that could lead to problems later on. Putting your requirements in writing should assure consistency and should avoid the accidental omission of any services.

It is likely that you will need to identify several organizations or individuals who can provide this expertise as a group. For these groupings to work effectively, you will need to supply project-related orientation and training to everyone involved.

6.4. Larger enterprises as models

If no large or medium-size businesses in the country or community have substance abuse prevention programmes, it is likely that the business community believes that these problems should be dealt with by the broader community and not in the workplace. You will then find it extremely difficult to convince small business owners/managers that they need to address substance abuse problems in their workplaces.

You will find it much easier to recruit small businesses for your project if you choose locations where at least a few businesses of any size already have substance abuse programmes, so that you can refer to them as examples.

7. Putting in place the project leadership

7.1. The host organization

The host organization is the entity that is sponsoring your project. It can be a government agency, an employers' organization, a workers' organization or a non-governmental organization (NGO). Whatever the nature of the host organization, it must have some experience of working with small businesses, understand their issues and have sufficient influence to give the project visibility and credibility in the small business community.

A host organization must also ensure that the project is adequately funded. It may provide direct funding or in-kind resources, solicit funds from other organizations, or any combination of these services. A national government entity, for example, could support the project through national and regional staff time, travel and meeting expenses, funds for materials development or through its prior experience in developing substance abuse prevention programmes with large corporations and businesses. Other types of organizations could offer access to their offices or might be able to provide trainers with experience of other small business initiatives.

The organization must be stable enough to function as the host for the entire duration of the project and also to provide a home for, and long-term support to, the programme once it has come to an end. Above all, it must be committed to the project's aims, that is, motivating small business owners/managers to implement workplace substance abuse prevention initiatives.

7.2. The project manager

The project manager is the person who is in charge of the planning and implementation of the project.

Good project management skills are the key to success in the implementation of a project. They are essential if the project manager is to grasp quickly the sense of the project and put in place the necessary systems and procedures. Although some knowledge and experience in workplace substance abuse programming and the operation of small businesses are certainly desirable, a person with a high level of project management skills, even if developed in another field, will probably be able to pick up quickly the basics of workplace substance abuse and small businesses and hire experts in those areas. However, when project management skills are weak, ineffectiveness and inefficiency will result.

The following is a list of the roles, responsibilities and qualities of a good project manager. Although it is probably unrealistic to expect a project manager to have all these skills, the list does serve to demonstrate the breadth and complexity of project management.

Roles of a successful project manager	Skills of a successful project manager. Able to:	Qualities of a successful project manager
• facilitator	• negotiate	• non-judgemental
• counsellor/mentor	• communicate	• open
• coordinator	• organize	• tolerant
• resource provider	• resolve conflict	• patient
• sounding board	• develop plans of action	• flexible
• problem solver/firefighter	• work with people on different levels	• open to constructive feedback
• motivator	• participate in and chair meetings	• realistic
• negotiator	• write (agendas, minutes, letters and reports)	• honest
• critic	• manage finances	• empathetic
• planner	• motivate people	• punctual
• trainer	• network	• tenacious
• presenter	• work in partnerships	• conscientious
• peacemaker	• think strategically and critically	• self-confident
• organizer	• exercise tact	
• positive role model	• be assertive	
	• coordinate	
	• control	
	• build teams	
	• manage stress	

7.3. The project advisory board

The PAB is a body made up of government, business and workers' representatives as well as representatives from other relevant groups, such as subject matter experts and NGOs. The PAB is an essential project component; its contributions can be extremely positive and its members should be active players in the design and implementation of the project and should be given the responsibility of assisting the project manager in recruiting small enterprises to participate in the project.

The PAB has two main aims:

• to provide advice and support to the project manager; and

• to provide legitimacy and credibility to the project in the eyes of the community, small businesses and the organizations which support them.

It is important that the PAB members are carefully chosen and that their functions and roles are clearly understood. Otherwise, the PAB risks becoming a mere ceremonial body, and the project will be deprived of the valuable contacts and credibility that PAB members can provide and of their help in gaining the support of individuals and organizations that can contribute to sustaining the project's activities.

Functions: The specific functions of PAB members can include the following:

• providing information, referrals and perspectives;

• making up for the lack of skills, expertise and specialized knowledge, particularly in the areas of small business and substance abuse;

• representing the interests of various sectors involved in the project;

- developing strategies on the overall approach of the project and working with the project manager to solve problems that arise during the course of the project;
- monitoring and discussing progress;
- using their influence within the community to heighten the status of the project, develop useful contacts and access expertise and funding; and
- assisting with assessment and evaluation.

Membership: To create an effective PAB, the organizations and individuals invited to be members must be able to fulfil one or more of the roles identified above. The primary areas of influence and knowledge of the PAB members should be within the substance abuse prevention and business communities. Most of the members should fit this profile. You may, however, want to include a small number of individuals or organizations as members who, although they have no background in the project's subject matter, are able to raise the project's visibility and influence funding, legislation and other community leaders. If the appropriate organizations and individuals are not recruited, the PAB can itself become an obstacle.

PAB members should be politically well placed, so that they can influence legislation and governmental budgeting and priorities. It is also essential that they be interested in the project and be committed to working towards achieving the set objectives according to the time they can devote to the project.

Recruiting and using the PAB: The initial impression you make can substantially affect the outcome of your efforts. From the start, you must give an air of professionalism and competence and generate enthusiasm.

As soon as potential organizations and individuals have been identified, each person should be approached personally and individually. This can be done either by making an appointment to meet the potential member or by sending a personalized letter of invitation that gives information about the project and the PAB and requests a meeting to discuss them further.

Since these individuals are likely to receive many requests to serve on boards and in community groups, the information that you initially provide must capture their interest and clearly explain why participating in the project is important *to them* and not just to the project. The reasons will vary by organization and individual and may include the following:

- rendering a service to the community from which they draw their customer base and their future workforce;
- improving their image within the community;
- networking with other small businesses on workplace substance abuse issues;
- making the community aware of their products and services.

Before contacting anyone, you must be able to explain clearly the points listed below. You may also want to prepare a package of materials for each potential member, which should include the same information. Even if you have written materials, you must be ready to present and discuss these points without referring to them:

- the goal and objectives of the project and a draft strategy and workplan to achieve the goal and objectives;
- the purpose and functions of the PAB, as well as the proposed meeting schedule;
- the support that the project will provide to the PAB; and
- the expectations of all PAB members (for example, the ability and the willingness to remain on the PAB for the entire duration of the project; attendance at regularly scheduled and, to the degree possible, ad hoc meetings).

The specific reasons for inviting each person or organization to become a member, such as their particular expertise and the functions they will be asked to perform, will differ.

Under certain circumstances, it may be necessary to reimburse members for certain expenses, such as travel costs, which are related to their service on the PAB. It may also be appropriate to offer refreshments before or after meetings, which will encourage networking and discussion. Whether PAB members should be reimbursed for their time or paid a fee for their services will depend on the existing rules, regulations and customs of the host organization.

As with your initial contact at the recruiting stage, the substance and tone of the first PAB meeting will greatly influence the members' opinion of the project and their willingness to continue serving. Again, professionalism and competence are key.

Topics for discussion and decision-making at the first meeting could include:

- the designation of a PAB chair;
- the finalization of the statement of purpose and the functions of the PAB;
- PAB membership, including identifying other individuals or groups that may be needed as members or advisers and the roles they will fulfil;
- rules and procedures of the PAB, such as the need for regular attendance at meetings and continuity of membership; and
- your functions as project manager in terms of the operations of the PAB.

The preparation of the minutes of this meeting is particularly important as they will set the parameters for the future operation of the PAB.

The role of the project manager vis-à-vis the PAB: Inasmuch as the PAB is an advisory body to the project and to you as project manager, it is not appropriate for you to be a member of the PAB. Rather, your role is to serve as the secretariat to the PAB by performing the following tasks:

- establishing a regular schedule for PAB meetings based on input from the PAB;
- establishing a draft agenda for each meeting in cooperation with the PAB chair;
- preparing a report on the status of the project that identifies progress made, problems encountered and how these problems are being dealt with;
- notifying each PAB member of the next meeting and distributing a draft agenda, draft minutes of the previous meeting and your report on the status of the project (to improve attendance you may want to send out more than one reminder of a forthcoming meeting); and
- taking notes during the PAB meeting and preparing draft minutes of the meeting, which document the decisions made and the action that you and the PAB members will take.

7.4. The project vision

Every project has a vision. Sometimes it is called a long-term objective or a goal. Whatever you decide to call it, the vision describes what should happen as a result of the project. It drives the project structure and the key decisions that will be made, and is what remains when the project has been completed, in other words, its legacy.

The project's vision should relate to the concerns and needs of the country or community in which you are working. It must be clear, otherwise key players will have trouble understanding the approach and structure of the project. This understanding is critical if they are to develop a plan of action that will achieve the project's objectives. The vision must be supported by the host organization, the project manager and the PAB. It should be documented so that everyone understands it and is working towards the same goals.

By way of example, the vision of the ILO pilot project, *Mobilizing Small Businesses to Prevent Substance Abuse*, was reflected in its document's objectives. The project's long-term objective was to prevent and reduce substance abuse and improve the health, safety and welfare of workers and their families. There were also two intermediate objectives: first, that by the end of the project, it was hoped that the necessary administrative, technical and resource capabilities would be established in each participating country and that a general model on drug abuse prevention in small businesses would have been adopted to support the small business community to develop similar programmes worldwide; second, that drug prevention strategies and programmes would become integrated into the other management practices of the participating enterprises.

8. Defining the project structure

This chapter lists the essential steps that need to be taken before you begin contacting small business owners/managers. Unless the materials and procedures have been carefully developed before you set your project in motion, you will put yourself at a big disadvantage: you may lose momentum and the interest of the small business owner/manager; and, far worse, you may lose credibility and fail to achieve the goals of the project.

8.1. Research

To develop a realistic project structure as well as effective recruitment and awareness initiatives, it is essential to collect as much information as you can about small businesses in general and their perceptions and needs related to substance abuse in particular. Well-planned research will provide this information.

For many people, research means statistics: lists of numbers, tables, charts and graphs. In most countries, some statistical data may be available on the incidence and prevalence of alcohol and drug abuse in the general population and on its impact on the economy at the national level. In some countries, this information may also be available for the large cities. Data related to workplace substance abuse are much scarcer. There may be some information available at the national level or for major international corporations. However, in most countries these data are unavailable and not collectable, even at the national level and certainly not at the local level.

So don't spend a lot of time looking for information that doesn't exist; use whatever is readily available and move on to uncovering collectable kinds of information. It is important to remember that information about what other small businesses are doing, especially small businesses in the same line of work, will be of most interest to small business owners/managers.

Having access to a research consultant or organization that can provide guidance and assistance could be a lifesaver. If your budget is tight, try contacting local colleges or universities to see whether a student or professor would be interested in doing the research.

First of all you will need information on the following:

- the prevailing laws and regulations of the community in which your project will operate;
- the values and attitudes of the culture and community towards alcohol and drug use; and
- issues of importance to the community that you can link to the substance abuse prevention campaign and that will make the campaign more relevant to small business owners/managers (HIV/AIDS prevention is a good example.).

Any information that you can find on the following topics may also be useful:

- substance abuse programmes and activities in other enterprises in the community, especially those in small businesses;
- the availability of substances of abuse;

- resources available to support your project (for example, subject matter experts, training facilities, professional substance abuse counsellors, treatment facilities);
- existing networks that might offer support; and
- existing initiatives that might complement your project.

The following information on small businesses should help you define your target population and then devise recruitment strategies:
- the location of small enterprises;
- the industries in which small businesses are found;
- groups that work with small businesses;
- the problems and external factors facing small businesses;
- networks or associations that represent small businesses;
- industries or occupations in which substance abuse may be of particular concern;
- what small business owners/managers think about workplace substance abuse;
- the kinds of assistance small businesses need on substance abuse issues; and
- the best ways to communicate with small businesses.

The sources and availability of information will vary from country to country and from community to community. You may be able to get information from the following:
- research institutions or universities;
- government departments, for example, health, welfare, statistics, labour, trade and industry;
- national councils;
- community-based organizations dealing with substance abuse;
- business groups, for example, chambers of commerce and industry, and trade associations;
- informed individuals and recognized experts;
- hospitals, clinics and treatment centres;
- census reports;
- unions;
- newspapers and magazines; and
- international organizations, for example, the ILO, the World Health Organization (WHO), the United Nations Drug Control Programme (UNDCP).

It is essential to find out how small businesses view the issue of substance abuse and what assistance they need in dealing with it. The information you gather on this may be primarily anecdotal and your best sources will probably be the small business owners/managers themselves.

To get hold of this information, you can send owners/managers a letter with a questionnaire, ask questions by telephone, or make an appointment to see them. You can convene a meeting of small business owners/managers to solicit their input. Generally, a personal approach works better. However, small business owners/managers are often reluctant to spend valuable time responding to questions, especially if they believe they do not have a substance abuse problem in their workplaces or that they should not interfere in the personal lives of their workers.

8.2. Key decisions

Geographic coverage

You may not be able to implement your project as extensively as you might like, since the resources available to the project will be the deciding factor in the number of locations you can serve.

Whether you are doing the research, orientation, recruitment, training and technical assistance yourself or recruiting and training others to do this work in the more distant locations, you will be using up a lot of resources. If you plan to recruit and train other people, you will end up travelling or paying to have them come to you for training. The more extensive the project, the greater the travel costs will be. In some countries, multiple locations mean multiple cultures and languages or dialects, requiring you to customize and translate your materials. In addition, you – and your resources – may be "spread too thin" resulting in less than adequate support for each location.

In order to reduce costs and stress levels as well as increase your chances of success, it may be preferable to choose a small number of carefully selected enterprises in a single geographic area. On a manageable scale, you can complete the entire project cycle, uncover any problems, and change your workplan and materials accordingly. Then, having perfected your project, you can use the knowledge you have gained and your successful outcomes to market it in other locations. You might even be able to find additional funding to continue and expand the project.

Business size

As already discussed in Part II, the definition of what constitutes a "small business" varies from country to country. At first, you will probably find it easier to recruit and work with businesses at the higher end of your small business size range. Once you have gained more experience, you can recruit businesses with fewer and fewer employees.

Number of participating businesses

As with geographic coverage, the level of resources is central to determining how many small businesses can be included in the project. As the number of businesses increases, the resources available for working with each small business will decrease, resulting in fewer awareness and training activities and less technical assistance for each small business.

The number of businesses in the project will be determined by the resources available to the manager in terms of staffing levels, funding and community support.

Recruiting a larger number of small businesses than the required target will cushion you should owners/managers subsequently drop out. However, in the event that no owners/managers leave the project, you must be prepared to work with all the businesses you have recruited.

Time frame

For a project to succeed, enough time must be allocated for its goals to be accomplished. A three- to five-year time frame is probably best.

The ILO pilot project, *Mobilizing Small Businesses to Prevent Substance Abuse*, put in place a time frame of three years, with the first year for planning and the second and third years for implementation. Towards the end of the third year, the evaluation of the project should be completed and the strategy for sustaining it implemented.

Introducing a new concept (substance abuse prevention) to a new audience (small businesses), with the intention of changing attitudes and behaviour that have been embedded in a culture for generations, cannot be done overnight. So don't underestimate the amount of time it will take for a substance abuse prevention initiative to become integral to the operation of a business.

Targeting small businesses

Based on your research and the key decisions that have been made on your choice of geographic area, business size and number of participating businesses, you are now ready to define your target group.

Select a group of small businesses whose owners/managers are motivated to take action and whose businesses are stable and financially viable. By finding small businesses that are most willing and able to act, you will improve your chances of success and create a cadre of small business owners/managers who can "champion" the project with their small business associates.

There are three general approaches you can use to identify your target group: by business sector, by shared location and by the suppliers and contractors to large businesses.

Business sector

If you can identify a business sector in which you can find a sufficient number of small businesses within your project's geographic area, you have an excellent opportunity to focus your project on that sector. If the sector is one in which substance abuse presents a significant hazard, such as transportation, chemicals or security, your entry to small businesses will be greatly facilitated.

- **Advantages:** Small businesses within the same sector have common concerns and share the same technical language. You will be able to confine your research to that industry and develop information and materials addressed to its specific needs in its "language", making them more relevant and interesting to the small business owners/managers. If the business sector has a trade association or other sector-specific business groups, you can ask them to send information on substance abuse in the industry to their members, encourage their members to participate and announce the project at their gatherings.
- **Disadvantages:** Companies may be too geographically dispersed, making it difficult to organize meetings, training sessions and seminars and provide technical assistance. Small business owners/managers may not want to discuss their experiences and problems with competitors in a seminar or workshop.

Shared location

A second method of identifying a target group is to find a specific location in which several small businesses from various sectors are situated. Examples include industrial estates or parks and shopping or commercial centres.

- **Advantages:** You could work with the recognized head of the industrial park who might actually recruit the small businesses and take care of the logistics of seminars and training for you. Logistically, it is easier to bring owners/managers together for meetings or seminars and to conduct awareness and training sessions for several owners/managers and workers from different small businesses at the same time. The small business owners/managers will share a sense of community and have a common interest in implementing a substance abuse prevention programme.
- **Disadvantages:** The concerns and problems of owners/managers may be unrelated, making it more difficult to prepare activities and materials relevant to all the participants.

Suppliers and contractors to large businesses

If your implementation sites contain large businesses or corporations that already have substance abuse prevention programmes, you might be able to arrange to work with them in targeting small businesses. Most large companies have a number of small suppliers and contractors with whom they regularly do business. The larger firms may be willing to write to these small businesses, promoting the project and encouraging the owners/managers to participate. A large business might even be prepared to inform its suppliers and contractors that it will give preference to businesses that participate in the project and who then implement substance abuse prevention initiatives.

- **Advantages:** You will have an easily identified group of small business owners/managers that may rely for their very survival partially – if not completely – on work orders from the large business. The involvement of a large business will lend credibility to your project and provide an incentive for small business owners/managers to participate, and stay, in the project.
- **Disadvantages:** You may alienate other small business owners/managers within the community by providing a competitive advantage to a select group of small businesses at their expense.

The best of all possible worlds in terms of recruiting would be to target a small area such as an industrial park in which there were several small businesses in the same business sector.

Evaluation methodology

Evaluation should be an integral part of every project. The purpose of an evaluation is to determine whether the project is achieving the goals identified during the development of the project's concept. A good evaluation will pinpoint the project's strengths and weaknesses and indicate what steps need to be taken to improve its operation and impact. The evaluation methodology and instruments need to be developed as part of the planning process to assure that all the necessary information will be available for the final evaluation. They need to be designed with the specific target group in mind.

The way in which the project will be evaluated should be decided during the planning phase because the evaluation methodology will determine what information should be recorded during implementation. If the relevant information is not gathered early enough, the opportunity to conduct a meaningful evaluation may be jeopardized.

Project managers often go into a state of paralysis when it comes to assessing and evaluating their projects. You need to keep in mind that evaluating a project does not imply that either you or the project has a problem. You will need to learn to identify positive, creative feedback, which is directed at improving the project, and not to take comments too personally.

Process evaluation and impact evaluation are the two ways of evaluating a project.

Process evaluation, which is most frequently used, looks at what has been accomplished during the implementation phase. It provides information such as:

- the number and size of small businesses that participated in the project;
- the number and type of marketing activities that were carried out;
- the number of small business owners/managers reached through these activities;
- the number and kinds of resource materials developed and distributed;
- the number and topics of the awareness and education sessions and the number of owners/managers and workers who attended each session;
- the results of the questionnaires distributed at the end of awareness and education activities; and
- the number and demographics of owners/managers and workers who made use of the assistance services.

Impact evaluation explores whether the purposes for developing the programme have been met.

The fundamental goal of most substance abuse prevention projects is to:

- increase awareness of the impact substance abuse has on small businesses;
- increase people's knowledge about substances of abuse;
- reduce the number of accidents, the rate of absenteeism and the costs related to health care and workers' compensation; and
- improve worker health and safety, enterprise productivity and the quality of the product or service.

Baseline data need to be collected to measure the project's progress. External political, economic, social, personal or work-related circumstances may also have an impact on the project. For example, political instability, the death of a family member or a major accident at the worksite may need to be taken into consideration during the course of an impact evaluation.

Evaluations can range from the rigorous to the informal, depending on the resources available and the needs of the enterprise. If project staff and PAB members do not have sufficient expertise to conduct an evaluation, it may be possible to find the expertise in the community. Rather than contracting for an evaluation, a low-cost or no-cost alternative would be to see if a staff member or student at a local university would be interested in undertaking the evaluation as part of a research project or course credit.

Monitoring the progress of the programme implementation should be ongoing and can be a regular topic of discussion at PAB meetings. Sample evaluation questionnaires for the project manager, PAB members and owners/managers can be found in Annex III.

Sustainability

The last and most difficult phase of any project is to plan for the continuation of the programme or activities after the project has ended. This may be particularly difficult with substance abuse prevention projects, given the number of organizations and individuals involved and the resources needed to continue providing services.

There is no single best way of ensuring long-term sustainability. Given the unique nature of enterprise cultures, production processes, working conditions, workforce characteristics, facilities and resources, each project needs to develop its own sustainability strategy.

Integrating substance abuse prevention initiatives into the operation of small businesses is not realistic, since they normally lack resources and expertise. It is also difficult to create and sustain a separate entity that will continue the work of the project; the inefficiency and difficulties involved in dealing with small business owners/managers directly makes this option unrealistic.

ILO experience has found that the best way of assuring the continuity of a project is to integrate the programme into an organization that already works with substance abuse issues. The ideal scenario would be for the host organization to continue the work of the project after it has come to an end, especially if the organization has an ongoing substance abuse function and integrates the project into that unit. This works far better than if the project comes under the auspices of a business organization where the substance abuse prevention work is simply an "add on". If, however, the latter is the case, you might consider including organizations that can guarantee sustaining the project from the very beginning as PAB members or as providers of awareness activities, training or assistance.

9. Preparing for implementation

9.1. Project management

A project can be viewed as any series of activities and tasks that:

- has a predetermined lifespan;
- has specific objectives and outcomes to be achieved;
- has a defined budget;
- consumes resources;
- usually requires the skills, talents and cooperative efforts of a team of people.

To manage your project successfully, it is essential that you, as project manager, have a firm grasp of the project's vision and structure, your role and responsibilities and the scope of your authority.

- Be sure that you understand the "big picture" and keep it clearly in mind. This is necessary if you are to be able to split the project into smaller, logical units.
- You will be the person who brings the project to life and keeps it alive. Ask questions if anything is unclear.
- If you were not involved in developing the project's vision or structure, make sure you are given a realistic period of time to become oriented with the project and to meet the relevant people.
- All too often, project managers are given roles and responsibilities and are held account-able but are given very little authority to perform the work efficiently and effectively. Make sure that your authority is consistent with your roles and responsibilities.
- Clarify which decisions you can make and which require consultation – and with whom. You will be driving the process and cannot do so with the brakes on! If authorization is required, be sure to request it in advance.

As often happens, you may be responsible for managing other projects or you may have ongoing responsibilities for other unrelated work. It is, therefore vital that when you accept the position of project manager, you are realistic about your workload.

It is also helpful if you take sufficient time to find out and grasp the major issues surrounding substance abuse prevention and small businesses in your country and especially in your community. If you do not have any background in these areas, this newly acquired knowledge will help you communicate with your "experts". If you do have the necessary expertise, gathering this information will assure that your knowledge is up to date.

Before starting the project, take as much as time as you need on planning. This could include organizing support staff and facilities as well as equipment. Once these decisions have been made, you will be ready to develop your plan of action and supporting budget.

Support staff

Based on the complexity of the project, you have to identify the staff support you will need. If your choices are limited by political or organizational constraints or by the available labour pool, make sure that the host organization and the PAB are aware of the situation, its possible impact on the implementation of your project and your recommendations on how to improve your staffing situation.

Facilities and equipment

In consultation with the host organization and the PAB, you will need to identify your needs. This could include office space, furniture, computers and printers, software, photocopiers, communications equipment and capabilities (such as telephones, email, fax and answering machines), stationery and postage.

Once the support staff, facilities and equipment requirements have been identified, the next concern is how to get hold of them. The simplest – but most costly – way is to get them on the open market. A more innovative and less expensive way is to see if any of the PAB members can help out. For example, part-time support staff could come from one or more of the organizations represented on the PAB. The host organization could provide the office space and communications equipment. Furniture and office equipment could be contributed by some of the organizations. Businesses or organizations not represented on the PAB may be willing to provide office supplies or do printing in return for recognition of their contribution to the project.

However, the key to successful project management is developing a comprehensive plan of action and a supporting budget.

Plan of action

A plan of action identifies all the major tasks that need to be accomplished, the sequence in which they need to occur and the time frames in which they have to be completed in order to achieve the project's vision. The plan of action needs to cover the entire time frame of the project. See Annex IV for a sample plan of action.

First, you will need to make a list of every major task that has to be done and in what order it needs to be completed. Then you will need to break down these tasks into smaller steps, also properly sequenced, and estimate the time it will take to do each one. Finally, you can add up the time it will take to do each step to get a total.

The accuracy of your estimates and the comprehensiveness of your task breakdown will depend on your experience in managing projects as well as your subject matter expertise. You may wish to consult with experts in project management as well as workplace substance abuse and small businesses for advice.

Your plan of action needs to be as detailed as possible, so spend enough time on it. The following suggestions should help you develop realistic plans:

• Check dates to ensure that there are no public holidays or other events that will delay or interfere with implementing the plan.

• Determine what will be required to prepare for each activity and for reports after the activity.

• Make sure that the people who need to be involved in each activity are available and that enough travel time has been set aside.

- There should be a logical flow to the plan of action. Activities should build on one another to reach the ultimate objectives.
- Ensure that the work processes and outputs (modules, phases and stages) are of manageable size and addressed in a logical sequence.
- The time between activities needs to be long enough for implementation but not so long that momentum is lost.

Be prepared to re-plan work continually during the implementation stage to accommodate the need to make changes. When making any adjustments, you will need to examine subsequent tasks to determine whether they also need modifying.

Project budget

Developing the project budget is next on the list. Your budget needs to identify the amount of money to be allocated for the specific tasks and activities in your plan of action. The budget should cover the entire time frame of the project and distribute the funds to cover every task. All too frequently, money is allocated too generously to the first part of the project, leaving insufficient funds to cover the costs in the final period.

Although at this point the budget will be an estimate, it still needs to be as realistic as possible, reflecting specific costs at the time it is developed. Cost each of the activities and items in real terms, for example, check with airlines and hotels to find accommodation and travelling costs, the price of graphics and printing, the renting space for training.

If the amount allocated to the project is insufficient to cover all the identified costs, there will be two options left open. First, it may be possible to obtain additional funding for the project. However, if this is not the case, the project's structure or even its vision will have to be adjusted. This is a decision that should be made by the PAB, based on your recommendations. And remember, no matter how painful, it is preferable to "downsize" a project rather than to stop all activity half-way through because you have run out of money.

Project management also involves developing internal communications and administrative procedures. Coupled with good time management, these should help keep your project organized and on track.

Communications

You can never have too much information sharing. Therefore, it is essential to devise an effective communications system from the very beginning to ensure that all stakeholders know what is expected of them, know how the project is progressing and are aware of any changes made to workplans. Be sure that communications channels and the flow of information related to the management of the project are realistic.

Determine the channels of communication that you are going to use and make sure that they are as short and direct as possible. You must be clear on the format of communications that will be accepted, whether they be faxes, originals and/or email. Telephone calls are not recommended. If, however, you do find it necessary to use the phone, be sure to prepare notes to the file indicating the time, date and the decisions made of your conversations. Provide a copy to those who participated in the conversation and to anyone else who needs to be aware of the conversation and the decisions taken.

Administrative procedures

It is essential that administrative tasks associated with the project management are kept up to date. Major administrative tasks include:

Correspondence

Whether by letter, fax or email, correspondence is your lifeline. It keeps you in touch with the relevant people, enables you to communicate and fulfils the important function of motivating people and record-keeping. If you have trainers in the field, it is a good idea to stay in touch with them in whatever way possible. Putting down expectations on paper, ensuring that proper contracts are drawn up and disseminated and thanking people for input are basic ways of developing good working relationships and ensuring good results. It is often not possible to make direct personal contact with collaborators; good correspondence will go far in making up for this shortcoming.

Minutes

Write up the minutes of a meeting as soon as possible after the meeting has ended. They should include all the important issues that were raised, the decisions made and any items pending or deferred until the next meeting. If writing up the minutes is left too long, details may have been forgotten or you may find that they're not ready for the next meeting.

Calendar

Use a calendar or diary to keep track of work such as:

- when agendas and minutes for meetings are due to be written and sent;
- dates for meetings;
- when preparations for activities should start;
- when and to whom you made telephone calls and sent faxes, email and surface mail; and
- equipment, materials and supplies required for meetings and training events.

Formats

Develop formats for agendas, minutes, reports, faxes and emails, which you will find streamlines project administration.

Records

Keep receipts, invoices, audited reports and correspondence in neatly labelled files, and file all the paperwork to keep the work organized and easily accessible.

Time management

You are the linchpin of the project. Demands will be made on you by the host organization, the PAB, the small business owners/managers and the workers. There will be activities to conduct and reports to write. If the geographical area of your project is extensive, you will have to travel. With so many things to do involving so many people, good time management is critical – and essential to ensuring that your job is rewarding rather than overly taxing.

A project always takes more time than anticipated, so consider adding more time as a built-in flexibility provision. It is better to finish ahead of schedule than constantly to be trying to catch up!

If, during the course of your project, expectations change, budget projections are found to be inadequate or delays occur, make both the host organization and the PAB aware of the problem and involve them in resolving it.

If you make a mistake, acknowledge it, learn from the experience and carry on.

Finally, find a knowledgeable person to use as a sounding board or mentor. Managing a project can be extremely stressful, and the support, perspective and advice of an objective, experienced person could contribute considerably to maintaining your sanity.

The following tips should help you manage your time more successfully.[1]

Long-term

Monthly and weekly calendars are the essential first step. Each time you get a significant new task, enter it twice: once on the monthly calendar and once on the weekly calendar. This will allow you to keep track of your commitments and to see when the high stress times will be. You can then distribute your tasks and schedule the significant parts of future tasks for quieter times.

Weekly

Look at both the monthly and the weekly calendars. Prioritize items to meet immediate deadlines and relieve the burdens of forthcoming stressful periods. Also, mark items that must be dealt with at specific times.

On a daily basis

- First thing in the morning (or, if you are a night person, at the end of the day) look at your weekly calendar and make a list of things due that day and over the next several days. Include on this list the parts of larger tasks that you have scheduled for this period.

- Prioritize the items on your list, giving one asterisk (*) to things you have to do and two asterisks (**) to things that are high on the "should do list". You can mark three asterisks (***) on items that can be put on the bottom of the list for today or which can be deferred. Remember that sections of large projects assigned to these few days must not be deferred too often if the system is to work.

- Be clear about priorities. Spending too much time on one annoying little task to get it just right is foolish if it gets in the way of a major task. Also, not all tasks need be done equally well; be clear about the value of each task.

- Estimate the time needed for each task.

- Examine the fixed items on the day's schedule and fit in the priority tasks around those items.

[1] Adapted from *Time Management*, University Foundations Program, University of Nebraska-Lincoln Campus, United States (http://www.unl.edu/UFP/timemgmt.htm).

Hints

- Start managing your time before your workload becomes unmanageable. If you are ahead of schedule, you can always slow down. But if you fall behind, you will spend all your time trying to "catch up" and create additional stress for yourself.

- If you are always feeling under pressure and do not know where your time has gone, keep a log of your activities, preferably with entries every 15 to 30 minutes, for a week. Look at where the time is going and make serious assessments of what can be rescued. If there is no time available for reallocation, then you are over-committed and, in all honesty to yourself and others, you must step back from some commitments. Share the load and delegate if possible.

- Be assertive about saying "no". If you burn out or crash, you have done no one any favours. Failure to complete a task is stressful. If you cannot complete a task, do not compound your stress by failing to notify those who are depending on your work.

- Be realistic about how long a job will take and do not schedule too many things in one time period. This will only increase the stress you are trying to reduce.

- If periods of time become available and are too short to accomplish a priority task but long enough to do a task that has been deferred, do the latter. You can then free up a larger segment of time for future use.

- Put more burdensome tasks first and then reward yourself with more pleasant ones later.

- Establish a daily routine; it clarifies your expectations and those of your associates.

- Utilize your high energy times for significant tasks. Determine the level of precision needed for each task and allocate your level of effort accordingly.

- Stay focused on the current task. Don't worry about what has already happened or what may happen in the future. You control neither and the distraction makes you inefficient.

- Build in relaxation periods but schedule them so they serve your needs for a break as well as for relaxation. Use them as rewards for the completion of tasks.

- Check off completed tasks. This will remind you of your list but will also relax you as you see the list getting shorter.

- Before you call it quits at the end of the day, look at your long-term list. Determine if there is one more task you can do now that will not be overburdensome but which will give you some flexitime later.

- Set realistic goals. If you are working with others, keep any commitments you have made. The expectations of your associates should motivate you.

- Be assertive about your own agenda; say "no" and mean it.

Time management is no easy task. You do not want to be so inflexible that there is no room for the unexpected. At the same time, especially when you begin to take control of your time, you want to be assertive about protecting your agenda. However, successful time management is, without a doubt, an invaluable tool.

The following chart could prove useful.

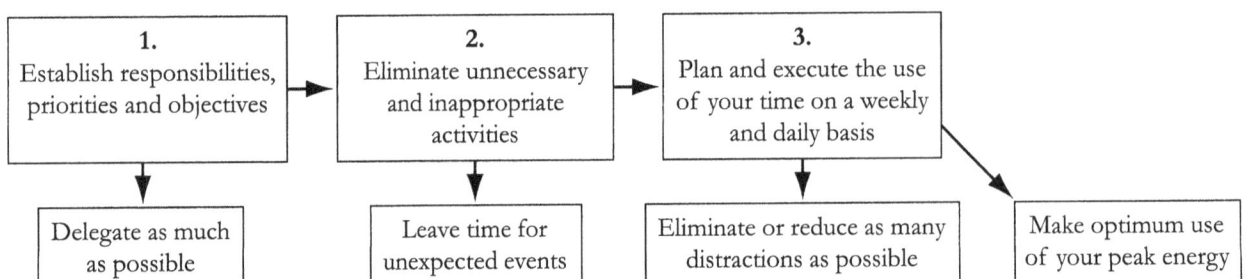

1. Establish responsibilities, priorities and objectives	→	2. Eliminate unnecessary and inappropriate activities	→	3. Plan and execute the use of your time on a weekly and daily basis
↓		↓		↓ ＼
Delegate as much as possible		Leave time for unexpected events		Eliminate or reduce as many distractions as possible / Make optimum use of your peak energy

9.2. Building networks

One of the most important tasks of the project manager is to build networks.

The composition of your network should be two-fold. First, it should include organizations or individuals, such as experts in workplace substance abuse and small business, trainers and substance abuse counsellors, who are capable of fulfilling the specific needs of your project and who have a grounding in the subject matter. They will be able to provide ongoing support, expertise and assistance during the course of the project. This is especially important if you lack expertise in any of the fields.

Your network should also include influential government, business, worker and community leaders. If you establish a network early on in the project, and especially if some of these leaders are on your PAB, designing a sustainability strategy should be much easier, as these key people will feel some ownership of the project, and you will avoid scrambling at the end of the project to find a strategy for continuing its work. If your project includes several geographic locations, you will need a comparable network in each location.

Local partners can make a huge contribution to the success of your project as they are already part of, and accepted by, the community. Valuable time and energy can be saved as they "open doors" based on their existing relationships. However, partners can sabotage a project, especially if they do not have a good understanding of its vision and objectives, are unclear as to their role and responsibilities, do not have sufficient information or believe that their territory is being invaded. It is, therefore, essential to establish good relationships with your network partners and especially with small business owners/managers. Much of the work of small business owners/managers is based on personal contacts, and the success of your project will depend on your ability to gain their trust and confidence.

9.3. Materials development

The information collected from your earlier research can also provide practical and useful ideas for developing and adapting materials for your project. Materials that are adapted to the target audience in terms of style, language and literacy level will prove much more effective than generic materials, especially those that were developed for a different culture and lifestyle.

The quality of the content and appearance of the materials will influence the way in which the target audience and the community perceive the project.

Materials development is a specialized task that can be expensive and time-consuming. Only experienced and qualified people should take it on. If a project staff member does not have this experience, you can enter into contracts with experts, providing that sufficient funds have been budgeted.

The resource materials should be simple, inexpensive and easy to read. Rather than preparing a brochure, consider developing an information item that an owner/manager or workers will have reason to keep around, such as a calendar, poster or computer mouse pad. Use plain language to ensure that all employees can understand your messages. It is important to remember that in some places literacy levels may be such that you should use pictures.

Of course, not all materials need be original. A lot of useful material can be found on the Internet, which, if it is not copyrighted, can be adapted or downloaded and used directly. What is essential is that the material is professional, respectful and interesting.

Before deciding who will reproduce the materials and how, explore the alternatives. Ask several printers to give you time and cost estimates. Get information on the different ways materials can be reproduced, such as photocopying and digital printing. Other issues to consider are the use of colour, illustrations and graphics. These can enhance the material but are costly.

Guidelines for materials development

- Identify target groups' needs and develop materials accordingly.
- Keep things simple, straightforward, easy to read and understand – materials should be concise, factual, objective and non-judgemental.
- Use language and pictures that are appropriate to the target group.
- Use graphics and illustrations where relevant.
- Establish themes and expand on them.
- Clarify concepts continuously.
- Put into user-friendly format (for example, small businesses usually have limited space to display information.).
- Be creative: use different approaches that will attract attention and make an impact.
- Test the concepts with the target group before finalizing the materials.
- Be open to suggestions, especially from small businesses.
- Avoid violent and moralizing messages and images that may be offensive to various groups.
- Take the time and trouble to make your materials practical – it is well worth the effort.
- Be aware of the different languages and dialects of target groups and be prepared to have materials in the different locations included in the project.

Use the media to increase the impact of your project. Appearing on local television or local radio, or getting articles published in newspapers and magazines will help get the message, of drug-free workplaces in general and your project in particular, across.

Resource directory

The resource directory is an essential project tool and should be ready before you start implementing your programme. Its purpose is to provide owners/managers and workers and their families with a list of qualified counsellors or programmes in the community that can help people with substance abuse problems.

In some countries, government departments or NGOs working in the field of substance abuse develop such guides. Otherwise, it may be necessary to develop your own resource guide for each location in which you are implementing your project.

A resource guide should contain the following information:

- the name of the resource and a contact person, address, telephone, fax and emergency numbers;
- a description of the services provided; and
- the requirements or conditions for use or access, such as health insurance, income levels and documentation of employment status.

Sample pages from a resource directory are reproduced in Annex V.

10. Implementing the project

10.1. Recruiting small businesses

The actual recruitment of small businesses is probably the most important task of the project – and possibly the most frustrating – as you will have to "sell" the need for substance abuse prevention programmes to often reluctant owners/managers.

Who should do the recruiting?

This is a decision you should make with the members of the PAB. Whether an individual or a team carries out the recruiting, the recruiter should be the person with whom the small business owner/manager identifies. Credibility with the owner/manager is, therefore, essential. The most effective technique is to invite a small business owner/manager who has implemented a prevention programme or a business leader who understands the value of substance abuse prevention to participate in recruitment activities. If they cannot participate in person, testimonials could serve as an effective alternative.

The affiliation of the designated recruiter can convey a subtle – or not so subtle – and unintended message to small business owners/managers. For example, if the affiliation is with a law enforcement agency, owners/managers may, despite what is said, infer a punitive aspect to the project. If the affiliation is with a government agency that has labour standards setting and enforcement responsibilities, many small business owners/managers will not participate for fear that the project is a way of inspecting the worksite for labour law violations. If the affiliation is with a treatment and rehabilitation centre, owners/managers may believe the project is just a ruse to fill more beds. A recruiter with a small business affiliation, for example, a well-known representative of the business community, will arouse the least suspicion.

Recruitment methods

There are several ways of providing information about the project to small business owners/ managers and inviting them to participate. Some methods work better than others, but much depends on the culture and environment. Some of the most commonly used methods are:

- word-of-mouth recruitment using entrepreneurs who attended earlier workshops, and referrals from various sources;
- advertisements in local newspapers;
- articles in local newspapers and trade newsletters; talks on radio programmes, especially those targeted at the business community;
- advertisements at seminars, trade centres and trade shows;
- structured recruitment visits by appointment;
- presentations at regular meetings of business groups that have small business owners/ managers as members; and
- meetings with leaders of various business associations to obtain their cooperation and support.

The recruitment message

Your first task will be to convince small business owners/managers that substance abuse in the workplace is a problem that should concern them and, perhaps more importantly, that it is something about which they can take practical, positive action. As one small business owner said, "Don't tell me about the problem. Tell me about the solution."

When making arrangements to meet the owner/manager, remember that many small business owners/managers do not have private offices. Alternative meeting space may need to be identified.

You will have to convince owners/managers that their businesses will benefit from participating in the project. Owners/managers who are seeking every competitive edge need to be made to understand that they cannot afford to overlook the importance of a healthy workforce, and one that is free of substance abuse. Other owners/managers will respond to messages about the health, safety and welfare of their workforce. Owners/managers who understand the advantages of having a substance abuse prevention initiative will be more likely to participate in the project. The message must be framed so that owners/managers do not see the project as simply another burden they have to bear.

Your second task is to outline clearly for small business owners/managers the purpose of the project, its goals and objectives, what they can expect from the project in terms of assistance and the cooperation and the action that will be expected of them. It is important to have a pamphlet containing this information available for each small business owner/manager. If there are no written materials explaining the purpose of the project and, in particular, the services to be provided and what is expected of the participants, the information given to the various owners/managers may differ, which may lead to problems later on.

The pamphlet should also contain information on how interested owners/managers can get in touch with project staff.

To a large extent, this initial meeting will be pivotal in the small business owner/manager's decision about whether or not to participate in the project. If it is not done professionally, the opportunity will probably be lost, as it is highly unlikely that the owner/manager will agree to a second meeting.

Once a sufficient number of small businesses have been identified, it is a good idea to meet each small business owner/manager personally to make sure that he or she understands the purpose of the project, the information and services that the project will be providing and his or her obligations. During this meeting, you can also solicit the input of owners/managers on drug and alcohol problems in their workplaces and what they would like the project to do for them. Based on the responses you get, you will be able to develop activities and provide assistance that responds specifically to their needs.

10.2. Developing a substance abuse policy

Most small businesses operate informally and lack any established management practices or written policies and procedures for any aspect of their operations. Many prefer to have nothing in writing, so that they can deal with problems as they occur and as they see fit. Therefore, the need to develop a substance abuse prevention policy can be a difficult sell. It may be more understandable and less threatening for owners/managers if you suggest that they develop a list of "rules", so workers will know what they can and cannot do in the context of substance use in the workplace and what will happen when they don't follow these rules. If the workers are illiterate, policies or rules will have to be read out to them and, if possible, presented pictorially or in signs.

A substance abuse policy is simply a description of how a company deals with alcohol and other drugs affecting the workplace. A workplace substance abuse prevention policy describes the "who, what, where, why and when" in a concise manner that everyone can understand. Usually, a policy for small businesses addresses the following topics:

- **Reason for the policy:** Small businesses will have different reasons for establishing a substance abuse prevention policy, such as worker health, safety and well-being; the health and safety of customers; product quality; or recent substance abuse-related incidents.

- **Coverage:** The owner/manager and the entire workforce should be covered by the policy. Indeed, the owner/manager should be seen to set an example. Depending on the work being done, there may be certain employees in high-risk jobs where the use of alcohol and drugs could be particularly problematic (such as those working with flammable materials or chemicals, operating motor vehicles, etc.).

- **Substances of abuse covered:** Depending on the substances that are being abused in a specific country, community or workplace and the rationale for having a policy, small business owners/managers need to decide which substances will be covered (for example, alcohol, specific illegal drugs).

- **Availability, possession and use:** The policy needs to state clearly when, if at all, substances of abuse can be brought into the worksite and which can be used during working hours, during breaks and at mealtimes.

Introducing a generic policy is a useful starting point, and can be discussed during training and orientation sessions. However, the substance abuse policy adopted by each small business should reflect the culture of the workplace and the needs of the owner/manager and the workers.

In most small businesses, workers are not formally organized. Owners/managers frequently make decisions affecting the business without any input from their workers. In the context of substance abuse prevention, you should encourage owners/managers to talk with their workers when they are developing the "rules". Employees are more likely to understand and accept the rules if they have been involved in their development. Sample policy statements can be found in Annex VI.

The policy statement is one area in which you may want to remain flexible. If you sense some reluctance on the part of owners/managers to adopt written substance abuse policies, insisting that they do so at the beginning of the project might be counter-productive. If these policies are perceived as impractical and unnecessary, the owners/managers might assume the rest of the project activities to be equally impractical and unnecessary and therefore lose interest. Actual programme implementation, through which the benefits are demonstrated, is a more effective starting point.

10.3. Awareness and training

A fair amount of awareness and training information and guidance can be found on the Internet, much of which is in the public domain. You can download and adapt this information and use it in your own project. There may also be sources of information and materials available from groups within the community that can be used, unchanged or adapted, to meet your needs. Don't be afraid to be creative and turn poorly presented information into great awareness and training materials.

Awareness

In most cases, a successful substance abuse prevention initiative changes attitudes and patterns of behaviour. Awareness activities can provide much insight into substance abuse and thus facilitate behavioural change.

Awareness activities in the workplace raise the profile of substance abuse as a personal, family and workplace issue. The purpose of workplace awareness activities is to increase the understanding of owners/managers and workers of how alcohol and drug use affects users, their co-workers, the workplace and their families and of what can be done when substance abuse is creating problems in the workplace.

Raising awareness is not a one-off event. Regular, ongoing messages will be more effective in creating awareness and supporting behavioural change than a one-off event, no matter how spectacular.

You will need to provide a variety of awareness activities to maintain a high level of interest. The kinds of information that can be the focus of individual awareness activities include:

- the physical and psychological effects of alcohol and drugs;
- the impact of substance abuse on family members;
- the impact of substances of abuse on the workplace;
- the signs and symptoms of substance abuse in the workplace;
- workplace rules or policy on substances of abuse;
- community resources where workers can get assistance;
- family and parenting issues;
- the existence of risk and protective factors related to substance abuse and dependency;
- the progressive nature of dependencies;
- communication and interpersonal skills;
- laws and regulations covering substance abuse in the workplace, especially for workers who drive company vehicles;
- coping strategies;
- the availability and use of self-help instruments;
- self-help groups; and
- the importance of supportive co-workers and families in changing patterns of behaviour and sustaining change.

Younger workers typically consume more alcohol, use more drugs and are more susceptible to peer pressure than more mature workers. In addition, they are more vulnerable than older workers to the effects of alcohol or other substances. Therefore, if you have any small businesses in your project with large numbers of younger workers, you might consider developing awareness activities that target this specific group.

Self-assessment tools can be especially valuable to workers who are beginning to have problems controlling their drinking. With these tools, employees can determine for themselves whether their use of alcohol or drugs is becoming a problem. If self-assessment information is easily available, workers have an opportunity to identify substance abuse problems at an early stage. The earlier a problem is identified, the easier it is to deal with. The CAGE assessment tool is easy to use and has proven to be very accurate in assessing alcohol abuse. This and other self-assessment tools can be found in Annex VII.

Employee orientation is a specific kind of awareness activity. Orientation familiarizes new workers with the way the small business operates, including its rules on substance abuse. In addition to providing written material to the new worker, an orientation can involve face-to-face meetings with owners/managers, who can provide more detailed information, clarify information and answer questions.

Encouraging your small business owners/managers and workers to become involved in substance abuse-related community activities can also serve to raise awareness. Furthermore, collaboration with community groups can strengthen both your project and prevention activities in the community.

Training

Small business owners/managers

In addition to the information on awareness activities that benefits employers and workers, small business owners/managers need information on how to deal with an employee who may have a substance abuse problem.

The role of the owner/manager is not to diagnose a substance abuse problem but to identify and address performance problems. These problems may be related to substance abuse or they may result from other medical or personal problems. However, it is important that owners/managers are able to recognize the signs and symptoms of substance abuse and then know how to deal with workers who may have a substance abuse problem.

When a substance abuse problem is suspected, the response of the owner/manager will largely depend on the available resources. If the community can provide counselling services, the owner/manager can refer the worker to the relevant groups. The owner/manager could also ask substance abuse professionals for help. However, if no such resources are available, the only choice left open to the owner/manager will be to discuss matters with the worker and encourage the employee to do something about any personal problem that might be causing or contributing to poor performance or unacceptable conduct.

You may also need to conduct special training sessions for owners/managers and workers to alert them to the greater risks of certain sectors and specific working conditions. In small businesses in which employees operate powerful equipment, work under extreme conditions or are responsible for the safety of others, the use of a psychoactive substance can be particularly problematic.

Training the trainers

If your project is implemented in several geographic locations or is so large that you are unable to do all the awareness and training yourself, you may need to select and train trainers to assist you. Being able to identify good quality trainers who will be the project's "face" and who will be responsible for presenting the information to the target groups is, therefore, critical.

You might consider using the following criteria when selecting trainers:

- knowledge of workplace substance abuse;

- knowledge of small businesses;

- experience in facilitating the group process;

- understanding the target group's dynamics;
- experience in using an adult training approach;
- availability (for the entire training process);
- an open and approachable manner;
- a non-judgemental attitude;
- knowledge of and commitment to the project and its goals;
- culture and gender sensitivity; and
- that they are comfortable working with people from different circumstances, levels of development, ethnic groups and religions.

If you are unable to identify trainers with both substance abuse and small business knowledge and experience, you could recruit co-trainers, one with a knowledge of small business and its dynamics and the other with a knowledge of substance abuse and its dynamics.

It is important to bear in mind the following:

- Small businesses probably won't have suitable training workspaces. You will have to find appropriate – and accessible – locations.

- Most small business owners/managers often cannot afford to release one, much less several, of their workers at the same time to attend awareness and training sessions. Keeping each session as short as possible and holding it during lunch or break periods, if workers are agreeable, will reduce the objections of owners/managers. Scheduling sessions before or after work will be more convenient for owners/managers, but is likely to be unpopular with the workers.

- When attempting to pull together a training group of sufficient size, assuring that the workers are at the same educational and knowledge levels, while preferable, may not be realistic. If, however, you are working with small businesses in the same business sector, workers across the businesses are more likely to have common backgrounds and interest levels.

Several excellent awareness and training activities and materials were developed by the National Project Coordinators (NPCs) in the ILO pilot project *Mobilizing Small Businesses to Prevent Substance Abuse*.[1] A few of these items will be available on the ILO website at: http://www.ilo.org/public/english/protection/safework/drug/index.htm

Some of the more creative workplace awareness activities included the following:

- a series of exhibition modules on different topics, from the organization and administration of the project to evaluation results;
- a "Walk Away from *Dadah*"[2] event, which attracted 2,000 workers and their families involved in the project;
- worker quizzes;
- family awareness days;
- community health fairs with representatives of community substance abuse and health-care facilities;
- street plays;
- videos; and
- a compact disc.

---

[1] The NPC in Malaysia was able to develop many training and awareness information and materials, since the National Drug Agency absorbed many of the costs associated with the implementation of the pilot project and money was, therefore, available for project materials.

[2] The Malaysian word for illicit drugs.

To raise awareness of the pilot project, NPCs engaged in or developed the following:

- television and radio interviews;
- newspaper articles;
- public service announcements; and
- websites.

The NPCs also developed several excellent training guides and manuals:

- *Interpersonal skills in drug abuse prevention* (Malaysia);
- *Stress management* (Malaysia);
- *Drug abuse prevention and refusal skills for workers* (Malaysia);
- *Parenting skills in drug prevention* (Malaysia);
- *Managing substance abuse in the workplace: Trainer's guide and participant's manual* (South Africa);
- *Manual on prevention of substance abuse in small enterprises* (India);
- *A manual on mobilizing small businesses to prevent substance abuse* (in Arabic, Egypt).

10.4. Early identification and assistance

Few workplaces have not had a worker with a substance abuse problem at one time or another. If the problem is affecting the ability of the worker to perform his or her duties, the employer has a limited number of ways to respond. Traditionally, there have been three options:

1. The problem can be ignored. However, dependency is a progressive health problem; alcohol and drug abuse usually gets worse so that costs will continue to escalate.

2. The worker can be fired. Although this may solve the immediate problem for the employer, there can be a number of direct and indirect costs to the employer, including the loss of a skilled worker and the time and the expense incurred in recruiting a replacement. The impact on the worker and family members can be devastating.

3. The owner/employer can try to help the worker with the problem. This can often do more harm than good, and the owner/employer may become so involved in trying to resolve the problem that it takes a significant toll on him or her and, potentially, on the business. Frequently, the worker does not get the assistance needed.

However, there is another path that can be followed. This is to offer or allow workers the opportunity to seek help for substance abuse problems without the risk of losing their jobs. The harmful use of alcohol and drugs usually takes a number of years to develop and, as the problem gets worse, the worker will rarely be able to deal with it successfully without some level of assistance.

The purpose of assistance is to interrupt the harmful use of alcohol and drugs so that the worker can adopt a healthier lifestyle and return to being a productive member of society. Being able to keep a job is often an important source of motivation for a worker to do something about a substance abuse problem. Providing or allowing workers with substance abuse problems the opportunity to get assistance is often less expensive that incurring the costs of continued poor performance, lost productivity, disciplinary action, job termination and the subsequent recruitment and training of another worker.

There are many levels of assistance. An assessment by a trained professional is necessary to determine the kind of assistance that would most benefit a worker. In some locations, community groups provide these services at no cost to the individual. Services may be available from private organizations, sometimes referred to as employee assistance programmes (EAPs). Sometimes, services are only available on a more piecemeal basis. Counselling and assistance may be available from treatment hospitals or government treatment centres. Contracts for assistance can be made with NGOs working in the substance abuse field. Obviously, the accessibility of services and resources will determine whether and what kind of assistance can be offered.

In some countries assistance is covered by national health insurance schemes. In others, employers provide health-care insurance to their workers. However, most small business owners/managers are unable to bear the costs of providing assistance to their workers. Some owners/managers may be in a position to allow a worker to take time off to participate in assistance programmes at full or half pay, or give unpaid leave.

In many communities around the world, Alcoholics Anonymous (AA) and other self-help groups, such as Narcotics Anonymous (NA), are the only resources available for dealing with alcohol and other drug problems (although AA does not regard itself as a treatment option).

If there is no local assistance available to small business owners/managers and their workers when a substance abuse problem arises, the ability of management to handle the problem constructively, even after having participated in the project, will be limited.

Testing [3]

Despite the increase in its use since the late 1980s, drug and alcohol testing in the workplace remains a sensitive and controversial issue, with much disagreement among countries, employers and workers about whether it should be done and, if so, how. There are also moral and ethical issues that should be taken into consideration when developing and implementing alcohol and drug testing programmes.

Most owners/managers do not use alcohol and drug testing in their small businesses. However, in some cases, especially when the health and safety of the workers or the general public would be at risk and when other means of identifying workers with substance abuse problems are unavailable, alcohol and drug testing could be used to identify those who may need help. When considering alcohol and drug testing, it is important to note the following:

- Drug testing does not assess the current impairment of a worker.

- An alcohol or drug test will not identify a worker with serious alcohol or drug problems who has not had a drink or used a drug just prior to a test.

- Testing programmes may raise important legal and ethical issues that need to be weighed.

- There are no common international standards and procedures for alcohol and drug testing.

If any of your small businesses are considering conducting alcohol or drug tests, the owners/managers should be aware of any legal limits that may exist in their countries. Testing for alcohol and drugs is not a simple process, and employers would be well advised to seek professional advice and assistance in developing testing programmes to protect their rights as well as those of their workers.

---

[3] An overview of different aspects and of internationally agreed guidelines can be found in *Drug and Alcohol Testing in the Workplace*. The report of an ILO Interregional Tripartite Experts Meeting, held in May 1993 in Oslo, Norway, *Drug and Alcohol Testing in the Workplace* (ILO, Geneva, 1994) contains more detailed information.

10.5. Concluding remarks

Small businesses are as individual as the people who own and run them. The guidelines of this manual have thus been developed accordingly and it is important to remember that the information provided can, and indeed should, be adapted to the specific circumstances and needs of each small business, taking into account the political, social, cultural and financial environments of the countries and regions in which the substance abuse prevention programme is being initiated.

Substance abuse affects communities throughout the world and no workplace is immune. Since the number of small businesses with substance abuse problems is growing and the use of alcohol and drugs in the workplace is having an increasingly detrimental effect on small businesses, urgent action is needed. As the more effective and less costly way of dealing with substance abuse, implementing a substance abuse prevention programme is clearly the best solution.

ANNEXES

Alcohol, alcoholism and alcohol abuse

Many people drink alcohol occasionally. Some drink moderate amounts of alcohol on a more regular basis. For women or people over the age of 65, a moderate amount means no more than one drink per day. For a man, this means no more than two drinks per day. Drinking at these levels is not usually associated with health risks and, in fact, can help prevent certain forms of heart disease.

Under certain circumstances, however, even moderate drinking is not risk free. At more than moderate levels, drinkers are at risk from serious problems with their health, families, friends and co-workers.

What is alcohol?	Alcohol is a liquid-distilled product of fermented fruits, grains and vegetables. It is used as a solvent, antiseptic and sedative. Alcohol has moderate potential for abuse.

Possible effects

- Intoxication
- Sensory alteration
- Anxiety reduction

Symptoms of overdose

- Staggering
- Odour of alcohol on breath
- Loss of coordination
- Slurred speech, dilated pupils
- Foetal alcohol syndrome (FAS), in babies
- Nerve and liver damage

Withdrawal syndrome

- Sweating
- Tremors
- Altered perception
- Psychosis, fear, auditory hallucinations

Indications of possible misuse

- Confusion, disorientation, loss of motor nerve control
- Convulsions, shock, shallow respiration
- Involuntary defecation, drowsiness
- Respiratory depression and possible death

Did you know that:

- alcohol is a depressant that decreases the responses of the central nervous system?
- excessive drinking can cause liver damage and psychotic behaviour?
- as little as two beers or drinks can impair coordination and thinking?
- alcohol is often used by substance abusers to enhance the effects of other drugs?
- alcohol continues to be the most frequently abused substance among young adults?

The impact of alcohol

Drinking and driving

Even a very small amount of alcohol can impair a person's ability to drive safely. Certain driving skills, such as steering a car while responding to changes in traffic, can be affected by BACs as low as 0.02 per cent. A 160-pound (72 kg) man will have a BAC of about 0.04 per cent one hour after having consumed two 12-ounce (354.8 ml) beers on an empty stomach.

Interactions with medications

Alcohol interacts negatively with more than 150 medications. For example, taking antihistamines for a cold or allergy and drinking alcohol will increase the drowsiness caused by the medication, making driving or operating machinery even more hazardous.

Interpersonal problems

The more a person drinks, the greater the potential for problems at home, at work, with friends and even with strangers. These problems may include:

- arguments with or estrangement from one's spouse and other family members;
- strained relations with co-workers;
- increasingly frequent absences from work or lateness in arriving;
- loss of employment due to decreased productivity;
- committing or being the victim of violence.

Alcohol-related birth defects

Alcohol can cause a range of birth defects, the most serious being FAS. Children born with alcohol-related birth defects can have lifelong learning and behavioural problems. FAS symptoms include physical abnormalities, mental impairment and behavioural problems. Women can prevent alcohol-related birth defects by abstaining from alcohol during pregnancy.

Long-term health problems

Some problems, like those mentioned above, can occur after drinking over a relatively short period of time. However, serious health problems can develop more gradually from long-term drinking, and women may develop alcohol-related health problems after consuming less alcohol than men over a shorter period of time. Alcohol affects many organs in the body and can increase the risk of the following diseases:

- **Alcohol-related liver disease:**
  Alcoholic hepatitis, or inflammation of the liver. Symptoms include fever, jaundice (abnormal yellowing of the skin, eyeballs and urine) and abdominal pain. Alcoholic hepatitis can cause death if drinking continues. If drinking stops, the condition can be reversed.
  Alcoholic cirrhosis, or scarring of the liver. About 10 to 20 per cent of heavy drinkers develop alcoholic cirrhosis, which can cause death if drinking continues. Although cirrhosis is not reversible, if drinking stops, the chances of survival increase considerably, people often feel better and liver function can improve.
- **Heart disease**, including high blood pressure and some kinds of stroke.
- **Cancer**, especially cancer of the oesophagus, mouth, throat and voice box, and possibly cancer of the colon and rectum. Women are at a slightly increased risk of developing breast cancer if they have two or more drinks per day.
- **Pancreatitis**, or inflammation of the pancreas. The pancreas helps to regulate the body's blood sugar levels by producing insulin and has a role in digesting food. Pancreatitis is associated with severe abdominal pain and weight loss, and can be fatal.

Alcoholism and alcohol abuse

For many people, the facts about alcoholism are unclear. What is alcoholism? How does it differ from alcohol abuse?

For most people who drink, alcohol is a pleasant accompaniment to social activities. Moderate alcohol use is not harmful for most adults. Nonetheless, a large number of people get into serious trouble because of their drinking. In many cases the consequences of alcohol misuse are life threatening, and the costs in human terms cannot be calculated.

What is alcoholism?

Alcoholism, also known as "alcohol dependence", is a health problem that includes four symptoms:

- **Craving:** a strong need or compulsion to drink;
- **Loss of control:** the inability to limit one's drinking on any given occasion;
- **Physical dependence:** withdrawal symptoms, such as nausea, sweating, shakiness and anxiety, occur when alcohol use is stopped after a period of heavy drinking;
- **Tolerance:** the need to drink greater amounts of alcohol in order to "get high".

Many people do not understand why an alcoholic can't just "use a little willpower" to stop drinking. Alcoholism, however, has little to do with willpower. Alcoholics are in the grip of a powerful "craving" or uncontrollable need for alcohol that overrides their ability to stop drinking. This need can be as strong as the need for food or water.

Although some people are able to recover from alcoholism without help, most alcoholics need assistance. With treatment and support, many individuals are able to stop drinking and rebuild their lives.

Some individuals can consume alcohol without problems but others cannot. One important reason for this has to do with genetics. Scientists have found that having an alcoholic family member makes it more likely that, if you choose to drink, you too may develop alcoholism. Genes, however, are not the whole story. Scientists now believe that certain environmental factors influence whether a person with a genetic risk for alcoholism will develop the health problem or not. The risk of developing alcoholism can increase based on how and where a person lives; family, friends and culture; and even how easy it is to get alcohol.

What is alcohol abuse?

Alcohol abuse differs from alcoholism in that it does not include an extremely strong craving for alcohol, loss of control over drinking or physical dependence. Alcohol abuse is defined as a pattern of drinking that results in one or more of the following situations within a 12-month period:

- failure to fulfil major work, school or home responsibilities;
- drinking in situations that are physically dangerous, such as while driving a car or operating machinery;
- having recurring alcohol-related legal problems, such as being arrested for driving under the influence of alcohol or for physically hurting someone while drunk;
- continued drinking, despite having ongoing relationship problems that are caused or worsened by drinking.

Psychoactive substances of abuse

A psychoactive substance is any substance that people take to change the way they feel, think or behave. This includes alcohol and natural and manufactured drugs. In the past, most drugs were made from plants, such as the coca bush for cocaine, opium poppies for heroin and cannabis for hashish or marijuana. Now drugs are also produced by synthesizing various chemicals. Drugs can be ingested, inhaled, smoked, injected or snorted.

There is a tendency to present some drugs as less harmful than they actually are, without taking into consideration their long-term consequences and the effects they have on adolescent development, particularly on the development of certain critical functions (cognitive ability and the capacity to memorize).

Even the occasional use of marijuana affects cognitive development and short-term memory. In addition, the effects of marijuana on perception, reaction and the coordination of movements can result in accidents. Ecstasy has been presented as having little or no side effects, but studies show that its use alters, perhaps permanently, certain brain functions and also damages the liver and other body organs.

Although not regarded as illicit, inhalants are widely abused. Some of these volatile substances, which are present in products such as glue, paint, gasoline and cleaning fluids, are directly toxic to the liver, kidney or heart. Some produce progressive brain degeneration. Inhalants may cause loss of muscle control; slurred speech; drowsiness or loss of consciousness; excessive secretions from the nose and watery eyes; and damage to the brain and lung cells.

The major problem with psychoactive drugs is that when people take them, they focus on the desired mental and emotional effects and ignore the potentially damaging physical and mental side effects that can occur. No illicit drug can be considered "safe". In one way or another, psychoactive substances alter the normal functioning of the human body and, in the long run, their use can cause serious damage.

There are five categories of drugs: narcotics, depressants, stimulants, hallucinogens and cannabis.

Narcotics

What are narcotics?	• Drugs used medicinally to relieve pain • High potential for abuse • Cause relaxation with an immediate "rush" • Initial unpleasant effects – restlessness, nausea
Possible effects	• Euphoria • Drowsiness, respiratory depression • Constricted (pinpoint) pupils
Symptoms of overdose	• Slow, shallow breathing, clammy skin • Convulsions, coma, possible death

Withdrawal syndrome	• Watery eyes, runny nose, yawning, cramps • Loss of appetite, irritability, nausea • Tremors, panic, chills, sweating
Indications of possible misuse	• Scars (tracks) caused by injections • Constricted (pinpoint) pupils • Loss of appetite • Sniffles, watery eyes, cough, nausea • Lethargy, drowsiness, nodding • Syringes, bent spoons, needles, etc.
Selected narcotic drugs	• Codeine • Fentanyl • Heroin • Opium

Depressants

What are depressants?	• Drugs used medicinally to relieve anxiety, irritability, and tension • High potential for abuse, development of tolerance • Produce state of intoxication similar to that of alcohol • Combined with alcohol, effects increase, risks multiply.
Possible effects	• Sensory alteration, anxiety reduction and intoxication • Small amounts cause calmness, relaxed muscles. • Larger amounts cause slurred speech, impaired judgement and loss of motor coordination. • Very large doses may cause respiratory depression, coma and death. • Newborn babies of abusers may show dependence, withdrawal symptoms, behavioural problems and birth defects.
Symptoms of overdose	• Shallow respiration, clammy skin, dilated pupils • Weak and rapid pulse, coma, death
Withdrawal syndrome	• Anxiety, insomnia, muscle tremors, loss of appetite • Abrupt cessation or reduced high dose may cause convulsions, delirium and death.
Indications of possible misuse	• Behaviour similar to alcohol intoxication (without odour of alcohol on breath) • Staggering, stumbling, lack of coordination, slurred speech • Falling asleep while at work, difficulty concentrating • Dilated pupils
Selected depressant drugs	• Amobarbital • Benzodiazeprine • Diazepam • Methaqualone • Nitrous oxide • Pentobarbital

Stimulants

What are stimulants?	• Drugs used to increase alertness, relieve fatigue and to make a person feel stronger and more decisive
	• Used for euphoric effects or to counteract the down feeling of tranquillizers or alcohol
Possible effects	• Increased heart and respiratory rates, elevated blood pressure, dilated pupils and decreased appetite
	• High doses may cause rapid or irregular heartbeat, loss of coordination and collapse.
	• May cause perspiration, blurred vision, dizziness, a feeling of restlessness, anxiety, delusions.
Symptoms of overdose	• Agitation, increase in body temperature, hallucinations, convulsions, possible death
Withdrawal syndrome	• Apathy, long periods of sleep, irritability, depression, disorientation
Indications of possible misuse	• Excessive activity, talkativeness, irritability and argumentativeness or nervousness
Selected stimulant drugs	• Amfetamine
	• Benzedrine
	• Benzfetamine
	• Butyl nitrite
	• Cocaine
	• Crack (the crystalline form of cocaine)
	• Dextroamfetamine
	• Ice (the crystalline, smokeable form of methamfetamine)
	• Methamfetamine
	• Methylphenidate
	• Phenmetrazine

Did you know that:

- a cocaine "high" lasts from between five to 20 minutes?
- cocaine use may cause severe "mood swings" and irritability?
- you need more and more cocaine each time you want a "high"?
- cocaine increases your blood pressure and heart rate, which is particularly dangerous if you have a heart condition?
- a single dose can cause death?
- possession and use are illegal and can result in fines and arrest?

Did you know that:

- crack is almost instantly addictive?
- a single dose could cause a fatal heart attack?
- repeated use may cause insomnia, hallucinations, seizures and paranoia?
- the euphoric effects of crack last only a few minutes?
- there are more hospitalizations per year resulting from crack and cocaine use than from any other illicit substances?

Did you know that:

- ice is extremely addictive – sometimes after just one dose?
- ice can cause convulsions, heart irregularities, high blood pressure, depression, restlessness, tremors and severe fatigue?
- an overdose can cause coma and death?
- when you stop using ice, you may experience deep depression?
- ice causes a very jittery "high", along with anxiety, insomnia and sometimes paranoia?

Hallucinogens

What are hallucinogens?	• Drugs that produce behavioural changes that are often multiple and dramatic
	• No known medical use, but some block sensations to pain and use may result in self-inflicted injuries.
	• So-called "designer drugs", made to imitate certain illegal drugs, are many times stronger than the drugs they imitate.
Possible effects	• Rapidly changing feelings, immediately and long after use
	• Chronic use may cause persistent problems including depression, violent behaviour, anxiety and distorted perception of time.
	• Large doses may cause convulsions, coma, heart and lung failure and ruptured blood vessels in the brain.
	• May cause hallucinations, illusions, dizziness, confusion, suspicion, anxiety and loss of control.
	• Can have delayed effects: "flashbacks" may occur long after use.
	• A single dose of a designer drug may cause irreversible brain damage.
Symptoms of overdose	• Longer, more intense "trip" episodes, psychosis, coma, death
Withdrawal syndrome	• No known withdrawal syndrome
Indications of possible misuse	• Extreme changes in behaviour and mood; a person may sit or recline in a trance-like state or may appear fearful
	• Chills, irregular breathing, sweating, trembling hands
	• Changes in sense of light, hearing, touch, smell and time
	• Increase in blood pressure, heart rate and blood sugar
Selected hallucinogens	• Bufotenine
	• LSD (Lysergic Acid Diethylamide)
	• MDA (Methylenedioxyamphetamine)
	• MDEA (Methylenedioxyethylamphetamine)
	• MDMA (Methylenedioxymethamphetamine)
	• Mescaline
	• MMDA (Methoxymethylenedioxyamphetamine)
	• PCP (Phencyclidine)

Cannabis

What is cannabis?	• The hemp plant from which marijuana and hashish are produced
	• Hashish consists of resinous secretions of the cannabis plant.
	• Marijuana is a tobacco-like substance.
Possible effects	• Euphoria followed by relaxation
	• Loss of appetite
	• Impaired memory, concentration, knowledge retention
	• Loss of coordination; more vivid sense of taste, sight, smell, hearing
	• Stronger doses cause fluctuating emotions, fragmentary thoughts, disoriented behaviour, psychosis.
	• May cause irritation to lungs and respiratory system.
	• May cause cancer.
Symptoms of overdose	• Fatigue, lack of coordination, paranoia, psychosis
Withdrawal syndrome	• Insomnia, hyperactivity, sometimes decreased appetite
Indications of possible misuse	• Animated behaviour and loud talking followed by sleepiness
	• Dilated pupils, bloodshot eyes
	• Hallucinations
	• Distortions in depth and time perception
	• Loss of coordination

Did you know that:
- marijuana can cause impaired short-term memory, a shortened attention span and delayed reflexes?
- taken during pregnancy, marijuana can cause birth defects?
- marijuana can cause a fast heart rate and pulse?
- repeated use of marijuana can cause breathing problems?
- marijuana can cause relaxed inhibitions and disoriented behaviour?

Sample evaluation questionnaires

The following questionnaires were used in the ILO pilot project, *Mobilizing Small Businesses to Prevent Substance Abuse*. Because of this, they make frequent reference to the national context, although they can be adapted for use in substance abuse prevention projects that are more local in scope. The annex includes:

- a questionnaire for NPCs (can be adapted for project managers);
- a questionnaire for National PAB and Steering Committee members (can be adapted for PAB members);
- an enterprise questionnaire (for owners/managers);
- a case study interview with enterprise owners/managers

Mobilizing Small Businesses to Prevent Substance Abuse/Project INT/95/M27/NOR
Questionnaire for National Project Coordinators

Name: _____   Country: _____

Role of the National Project Coordinator
The role of the NPC in this project included preparing workplans; establishing the Office of the NPC in the Host Organization; managing day-to-day operations; organizing training courses, seminars and workshops; preparing progress reports and documentation; drafting reports; compiling and producing resource materials; and, evaluation.

How well did the role of the NPC fit your situation and mesh with your other responsibilities? What is your evaluation of the role of the NPC? (Was it too broad, too narrow, or just about right?)

_____

_____

Planning and administration
At the beginning of the project, was it clear to you and other persons on the National Project Team that some of the small businesses in your country needed this kind of project?

_____

_____

Did you anticipate any difficulties in selecting small businesses and getting them to participate?

_____

_____

What percentage of your time was spent by you and members of the project management team on each of the following activities?

*Activity and approximate amount of time spent on each *

_____   discussions with the ILO and beginning the project; getting started

_____   delivering talks; attending meetings; seminars, training sessions, etc.

_____   reviewing information, discussions with other officials, coordination

_____   providing assistance to small business owners and managers in carrying out prevention

_____   trying to get small businesses to participate; contacts/discussions with small businesses

_____   discussing individual staff, employee, or family members' problems

* Each entry should be a percentage of the total. The six entries together should equal about 100 per cent.

Assessment

Before this project, do you think that most small business owners or managers recognized that there was a problem with alcohol or drugs in many enterprises in your country?

A. ☐ yes   ☐ no   ☐ not sure   B. If "yes", why?

_____

_____

What kind of assessment, if any, was carried out in your country, as part of this project or separately?

_____

_____

If no assessment was done, was there a description of workplace drug and alcohol problems available to you?

_____

_____

Purpose and Priority

During this project, was it clear what you and the national team were supposed to do to implement the project and how the project would help you to plan and carry out various activities?

☐ yes, it was very clear   ☐ clear for most activities, but not all   ☐ no, it was not clear

For most of the small businesses in your country, how important are the following kinds of problems? How much do owners/managers emphasize each of these areas in their day-to-day operations? For each problem area, enter a number that indicates your estimate of the degree of importance, the relevance, the priority for this area, as reflected _by the small enterprise owners/managers themselves._

Degree of importance
Enter a number from 1 to 6 below in each space in columns A and B.
1 = very important   2 = important   3 = low degree of importance
4 = not important/not a concern   5 = depends on each enterprise   6 = cannot say

A. What most owners/ managers actually do/ previous priorities	Problems for small business	B. What owners/managers should aim to do/ current priorities
	Theft and security	
	Smoking	
	Safety and accidents	
	Drugs and alcohol	
	Mental illness; depression	
	Gambling	
	Violence and serious conflict	

Selection and participation of small businesses

Over the entire length of the project, how many businesses participated, in any way, in this project? What do you estimate was the total number of enterprises that participated in any way in project activities?

_____

How many were active participants, stayed with the project most of the time, and tried to carry out some kind of prevention programme?

_____

Comment: _____

Were there some owners/managers who were reluctant to participate or felt that the project did not really have anything to offer them?

_____

Comment: _____

Did some small business persons think that a drug or alcohol programme was not needed or was premature?

_____

Comment: _____

Do you think that enterprises had enough exposure and time to take full advantage of the project? Did they have enough contact and time to absorb the ideas and take full advantage of them?

_____

Comment: _____

Implementation

To implement a prevention programme in businesses, various activities may be carried out. These activities are usually not of equal importance to all small businesses. How important were the activities listed below to the small businesses in your country? *For each activity listed in rows 1 to 6 below, indicate the degree of importance by adding a tick in one of the columns.*

Activity	Major importance	Minor importance	Not important	Other/ comment
1. Policy development				
2. Training				
3. Employee awareness or education				
4. Assessment of the problem				
5. Counselling or treatment				
6. Referral (for counselling or treatment)				

Resources

Were resources adequate to carry out the project?

A. ☐ yes   ☐ no   ☐ not sure; unclear

B. If "no", please describe the specific resources that were needed but not available:

_____

_____

Considering the technical advice provided to advisory groups and to enterprises, were there situations where additional information or technical guidance was needed but not available?

☐ yes   ☐ no   ☐ not sure; unclear

B. If "yes", please describe the specific areas.

_____

_____

Is there now adequate expertise in your country to design and operate prevention programmes for small enterprises without outside assistance?

☐ yes   ☐ no   ☐ not sure

If "yes", do you think that this expertise is available to small businesses? (more than one alternative may be ticked)

☐ yes   ☐ no   ☐ unsure   ☐ depends on the small business owner/manager

Achievement and impact

In general, did the project achieve the goals set out by the ILO and your country?

☐ yes   ☐ no   ☐ unsure

Comment: _____

Did the project have more of an impact on the national level than on individual enterprises?

☐ national level impact was greater   ☐ impact at the enterprise was greater

☐ the impact was about the same for both   ☐ difficult to tell; not sure

What were the two or three aspects of the project that seemed to have the greatest influence?

_____

_____

Are there specific changes, either at the national or enterprise level, that these aspects of the project brought about? What are these changes or indicators of any changes?

_____

_____

Do you think that the enterprises involved in this project would react to an employee with an alcohol or drug problem differently now than before the project?

A. ☐ yes   ☐ no   ☐ not sure; not clear   ☐ some yes/some no

B.   If "yes" or some "yes/some no", how does it differ *since* the project took place?

_____

_____

Sustainability

Are there government agencies, NGOs, or associations that have adopted or plan to adopt some of the practices followed in this project?

A. ☐ yes ☐ no ☐ not sure; not clear

B. If "yes", which agencies or organizations

_____

How likely is it that any gains or improvements made as a result of the project will be sustained? And over what period of time?

A. At the national level:
☐ very likely ☐ likely ☐ not sure ☐ unlikely ☐ very unlikely

B. At participating enterprises:
☐ very likely ☐ likely ☐ not sure ☐ unlikely ☐ very unlikely

Circle a number from 1 to 10 below indicating your estimate of the length of time any gains may continue in national level agencies or organizations.

shortest time								longest time	
1	2	3	4	5	6	7	8	9	10
(several weeks)								(several years)	

Recommendations

If the programme to prevent drug and alcohol problems is repeated in other small businesses in your country, what changes would you recommend to increase the likelihood of its success?

_____

_____

_____

_____

Thank you!

Mobilizing Small Businesses to Prevent Substance Abuse
Evaluation of Project INT/95/M27/NOR

Questionnaire for
National Project Advisory Board Members
and Steering Committee Members

Name: _____ Country: _____

Describe your role in the project. _____

_____

Planning and administration

1. At the beginning of the project, was it clear to you that some of the small businesses in your country needed this kind of project?

_____

_____

2. Did you anticipate any difficulties in selecting small businesses and getting them to participate?

_____

_____

3. What percentage of your time was spent by you and members of the project management team on each of the following activities?

Activity and approximate amount of time spent on each *

_____ discussions with the ILO and beginning the project; getting started

_____ delivering talks; attending meetings; seminars, training sessions, etc.

_____ reviewing information, discussions with other officials, coordination

_____ providing assistance to small business owners and managers in carrying out prevention

_____ trying to get small businesses to participate; contacts/discussions with small businesses

_____ discussing individual staff, employee, or family members' problems

* Each entry should be a percentage of the total. The six entries together should equal about 100 per cent.

Assessment

4. Before this project, do you think that most small business owners or managers recognized that there was a problem with alcohol or drugs in some enterprises in your country?

A. ☐ yes   ☐ no   ☐ not sure

B. If "yes", why?

_____

_____

5. What kind of assessment, if any, was carried out in your country, either as part of this project or separately?

_____

_____

6. If no assessment was done, was a description of workplace drug and alcohol problems available to you?

_____

_____

Purpose and Priority

7. During this project, was it clear what you and the national team were supposed to do to implement the project and how the project would help you to plan and carry out various activities?
☐ yes, very clear   ☐ clear for most activities, but not all
☐ clear for some   ☐ no, it was not clear

8. For most of the small businesses in your country, how important are the following kinds of problems? How much do owners/managers emphasize each of these areas in their day-to-day operations? For each problem area, enter a number under Columns A and B that indicates your estimate of the degree of importance, the priority for this area, from the perspective of small enterprise owners/managers.

Degree of importance
Enter a number from 1 to 6 below in each space in columns A and B.
1 = very important   2 = important   3 = low degree of importance
4 = not important/not a concern   5 = depends on each enterprise   6 = cannot say

A. What most owners/ managers actually do/ previous priorities	Problems for small business	B. What owners/managers should aim to do/ current priorities
	Theft and security	
	Smoking	
	Safety and accidents	
	Drugs and alcohol	
	Mental illness; depression	
	Gambling	
	Violence and serious conflict	

Selection and participation of small businesses

9. Over the entire time of the project, how many businesses participated, in any way, in this project? What do you estimate was the total number of enterprises that participated in any way in project activities?

10. How many were active participants and tried to carry out some kind of prevention programme?

11. Were there many that were reluctant or felt that the project did not really have anything to offer them?

12. Did some small business owners or managers think that a drug or alcohol programme was not needed or was premature?

13. Do you think that enterprises had enough time to take full advantage of the project? Did they have enough contact and exposure to project activities to absorb the ideas and take full advantage of them?

Implementation

14. To implement a prevention programme in businesses, various activities may be carried out. These activities are usually not of equal importance to all small businesses. How important were the activities listed below to the small businesses in your country? *For activities 1 to 6 below, indicate by a tick whether each activity was of major, minor, or no importance.*

Activity	Major importance	Minor importance	Not important	Other/ comments
1. Policy development				
2. Training				
3. Employee awareness or education				
4. Assessment of the problem				
5. Counselling or treatment				
6. Referral (for counselling or treatment)				

Resources

15. Were resources adequate to carry out the project?

A.   ☐ yes   ☐ no   ☐ not sure; unclear

B. If "no", please describe the specific resources that were needed but not available.

_____

_____

16. Considering the technical advice provided to advisory groups and to enterprises, were there situations where additional information or technical guidance was needed but not available?

A.   ☐ yes   ☐ no   ☐ not sure; unclear

B. If "yes", please describe the specific areas.

_____

_____

17. Is there now adequate expertise in your country to design and operate prevention programmes for small enterprises without outside assistance?

☐ yes   ☐ no   ☐ not sure

18. If "yes", do you think that this expertise is available to small businesses? (more than one alternative may be ticked)

☐ yes   ☐ no   ☐ unsure   ☐ depends on the small business owner/manager

Achievement and impact

19. In general, did the project achieve the goals set out by the ILO and your country?

☐ yes   ☐ no   ☐ unsure

Comment: _____

20. Did the project have more of an impact at the national level than on individual enterprises?

☐ national level impact was greater   ☐ impact at the enterprise level was greater

☐ the impact was about the same for both   ☐ difficult to tell; not sure

21. What were the two or three aspects of the project that seemed to have the greatest influence on enterprises and workers? (Example: repeating the prevention messages in different places in the factory.)

_____

_____

22. Are there specific changes, either at the national or enterprise level, that these aspects of the project brought about? What are these changes or indicators of any changes? (Example: workers talked about the different ways to manage the amount of alcohol they drink.)

_____

_____

23. Do you think that the enterprises involved in this project would now react differently to an employee with an alcohol or drug problem?

A. ☐ yes ☐ no ☐ not sure; not clear ☐ some yes/some no

B. If "yes" or "some yes/some no", how does it differ *since* the project took place?

_____

_____

Sustainability

24. Are there government agencies, NGOs, or associations that have adopted or plan to adopt some of the practices followed in this project?

A. ☐ yes ☐ no ☐ not sure; not clear

B. If "yes", which agencies or organizations

_____

25. How likely is it that any gains or improvements made as a result of the project will be sustained?

A. At the national level:
☐ very likely ☐ likely ☐ not sure ☐ unlikely ☐ very unlikely

B. At participating enterprises:
☐ very likely ☐ likely ☐ not sure ☐ unlikely ☐ very unlikely

26. Over what period of time are any gains likely to be sustained?
Circle a number from 1 to 10 below indicating your estimate of the length of time any gains may continue in national level agencies or organizations.

shortest time									longest time
1	2	3	4	5	6	7	8	9	10
(several weeks)									(several years)

Recommendations

27. If the programme to prevent drug and alcohol problems is repeated in other small businesses in your country, what changes would you recommend to increase the likelihood of its success?

_____

_____

_____

_____

Thank you!

Project INT/95/M27/NQR

Enterprise Questionnaire

Name of enterprise: _____

Postal address: _____

Tel: _____ Fax: _____ E-mail: _____

Name of person providing information: _____

Position of person providing information for enterprise: _____

This form is intended to be used by the national evaluator, who should fill it out during or after discussion or interview with the owner or manager of the small business. The content of the questionnaire should describe the drug and alcohol situation and reflect the views of the small business owner or manager. For each question, check the alternative that is closest to the owner/manager's views or write in the necessary information. Feel free to provide additional information or attach documents to clarify the answers. If a question is not relevant, enter "NR"; if the question is relevant but the information is not available, write "NA".

1. What are the main products or services of your enterprise?

_____

2. Indicate the number of employees of your enterprise at the end of 1998:

Full time_____ + Part time _____ = Total number _____

3. Is your small business a regular participant or member of any network, association or group of organizations that provide information, advice, or assistance to help deal with business or employee problems? (Examples: local business groups, Chamber of Commerce, trade associations.)

A. ☐ yes   ☐ no   ☐ not sure

B. If "yes", what network(s), association(s), or group(s):

_____

_____

4. Before your enterprise became involved in this project, did you have some kind of activity or programme to prevent drug or alcohol problems in your workplace?

A. ☐ yes   ☐ no

B. If "yes", what kind of activity or programme did you have?

_____

_____

Section I: Problem assessment

5. Before beginning your participation in this project, did you think that there was a problem with alcohol or drugs in your enterprise?

A. ☐ yes   ☐ no   ☐ not sure

B. If "yes", why?

_____

Section II: Participation

6. What did you think was the purpose of this project?

_____

_____

7. How were you approached to participate?

_____

_____

8. During this project, was it clear what you and your enterprise were supposed to do to implement the project and how the project would help you to plan and carry out various activities?

☐ yes, it was very clear   ☐ it was clear for most activities, but not all

☐ no, it was not clear

9. For approximately how long did your small business participate in this project?

☐ less than 6 months   ☐ 6 months-1 year   ☐ 1 -2 years   ☐ more than 2 years

Section III: Planning and organization

10. Was there any discussion of how the project should be carried out in your enterprise? (that is, were there any discussions to plan for the specific needs of your enterprise?)

A. ☐ yes   ☐ no

B. If "yes", how where you involved?

_____

_____

11. As a result of the project, did you prepare a policy on alcohol and drugs for your enterprise?

A. ☐ yes   ☐ no

B. If "yes", was the policy written?   ☐ yes   ☐ no

C. If "yes" does the policy concern: ☐ alcohol only   ☐ drugs only   ☐ both

D. If a policy has been prepared, how do employees learn about it?: (Describe how they may learn about the policy.)

_____

_____

12. Do employees drink alcohol at the workplace?

A. ☐ yes   ☐ no   ☐ not sure, not clear

B. If "yes", is this   ☐ rarely   ☐ occasionally   ☐ frequently

C. If "yes", please describe the situation:

_____

_____

13. What would be your small business's most likely response to an employee with an alcohol or drug problem?

_____

_____

14. Would your enterprise now react differently to an employee with an alcohol or drug problem?

A. ☐ yes   ☐ no   ☐ not sure, not clear

B. If "yes", how would the reaction differ?

_____

_____

Section IV: Implementation

15. Major elements of prevention and intervention programmes used in this project are listed below. Look over the elements and tick the "yes" or "no" columns for each element used. If "yes" is ticked, briefly describe how that element was implemented in your enterprise.

Element of the programme	Used in your programme? Yes	No	If used, how implemented in your enterprise
Policy development			
Training			
Employee awareness or education			
Assessment of the nature of the problem			
Counselling or treatment			
Referral for treatment			
Testing for drugs or alcohol in body fluids			

Section V: Technical guidance

16. Considering the technical advice provided to you, were there times or areas of the programme where additional information or technical guidance would have been helpful to your enterprise?

A. ☐ yes ☐ no ☐ not sure, not clear

B. If "yes", please describe the specific areas.

_____

_____

17. Do you now have the expertise in your enterprise to operate your prevention programme without outside assistance?

☐ yes ☐ no ☐ not sure

Section VI: Resources

18. What resources did your enterprise make available to your programme? (tick all those that apply)

☐ managerial/supervisory time ☐ employee work time released

☐ meeting rooms and equipment ☐ counselling or treatment services

☐ materials for training and awareness creation campaigns

☐ other (please describe)

_____

Section VII: Achievement and impact

19. Is any systematic information or data on alcohol or drug problems available both from before and since the project took place? (This could be information on any of the following areas: absenteeism rates, accident rates, disciplinary interventions (punishment or dismissal), qualitative atmosphere (team spirit, motivation, harmony), sickness and health-care reports, costs of health care, self reported changes in behaviour, productivity changes (products or services), employer initiatives to improve working conditions and offer leisure facilities or activities, worker initiatives to improve working conditions and "quality of life".

A. Is information available? ☐ yes ☐ no ☐ not sure

B. If "yes", was the information collected specifically for this project or was it routinely available?

☐ it was collected specifically for this project

☐ it was collected for other reasons

☐ it was collected both for this project and for other reasons

C. If "yes", please describe the information and indicate what the situation was before and after the project.

_____

_____

20. Has the situation with regard to drug or alcohol problems changed from the time before the project began to after it was completed? Have use or problems with use of drugs or alcohol increased, decreased, or stayed about the same in your enterprise?

☐ use or problems have not changed   ☐ use or problems have increased

☐ use or problems have decreased   ☐ we have no use or problems with use

21. The main objectives of this project are to mobilize enterprises and workers for the prevention and reduction of substance abuse in the workplace. How well were these objectives achieved in your enterprise? For a, b, and c below, tick one of the three alternatives to indicate whether the programme in your enterprise fell short, met or exceeded the objectives.

	Fell short of objectives	Met objectives	Exceeded objectives
a. Mobilizing enterprises and workers			
b. Prevention of substance abuse			
c. Reduction of substance abuse			

Section VIII: Sustainability

22. After the project ends, do you have plans to continue the prevention programme on drugs and alcohol in the coming year in your enterprise?

A. ☐ yes   ☐ no   ☐ not sure; don't know

B. If "yes", what are the plans?

_____

_____

C. If "no", why not?

_____

_____

D. If not sure or don't know, what is needed to decide whether and how the prevention programme will continue?

_____

_____

_____

23. If the programme to prevent drug and alcohol problems is repeated in other enterprises in your community, what changes would you recommend to increase the likelihood of its success?

_____

_____

_____

Section IX: Conclusions

24. What conclusions has your enterprise drawn about the prevention of drug and alcohol problems on the basis of your participation in this project?

_____

_____

_____

_____

25. Other comments:

_____

_____

_____

_____

_____

_____

Thank you for your information and your participation in this project!

Mobilizing Small Businesses to Prevent Substance Abuse
Evaluation of Project INT/95/M27/NOR

Case study interview
with enterprise owners/managers

Before the project began

1. First, tell me how you got involved with this project on alcohol and drugs? What were your first contacts and what impressions did you have at the beginning?

_____

_____

_____

2. Before you began to participate in this project, do you think that some small or medium-sized business owners or managers recognized that there were problems with alcohol or drugs in enterprises in your country?

A.   ☐ yes   ☐ no   ☐ not sure

B.   If "yes", why? What experience did some of them have that may have led them to think that there were problems with alcohol or drugs?

_____

_____

Participation

3. What was your understanding of what would happen in this project? Was it clear to you what you were supposed to do as a participant? How could the project help you to plan and carry out various activities?

☐ yes, it was very clear   ☐ clear for most activities, but not all   ☐ no, it was not clear

4. In your opinion, how important is the issue of alcohol and drugs for most of the small businesses in your country compared with other problems faced in many workplaces, such as theft and lack of security, lack of safety and accidents, mental illness, gambling, violence and conflict? How important do you think most small enterprise owners/managers think drugs and alcohol are compared with these other problems?

_____

_____

_____

5. How did you participate in the project? What specific activities did you or others from your enterprise participate in?

_____

_____

6. How did these activities have an impact on your enterprise? (Example: things learned; resource materials obtained for prevention; names of referral agencies obtained for future use.)

_____

_____

7. From going to the meetings and talking with other persons involved in the project, do you think enough small businesses participated in this project to make it really worthwhile in your country? What is your impression of the interest shown in preventive action on drugs and alcohol at the workplace? How would you describe it?

_____

_____

8. You probably saw several business owners/managers who expressed an interest and then did not continue their involvement. What were the main reasons for this, in your view? Did some of them feel that the project did not really have anything to offer them?

_____

_____

9. Did some small business persons think that a drug or alcohol programme was not needed or was premature?

_____

_____

10. Do you think that enterprises had enough time to take full advantage of the project? Did they have enough contact and exposure to project activities to absorb the ideas and take full advantage of them?

_____

_____

Implementation

11. Various activities can be carried out to implement a prevention programme in a small business. These activities will not, however, be of equal importance to all companies. What were the most important activities carried out by the project? What was done that was most helpful to you?

_____

_____

Technical guidance

12. Considering the technical advice provided to enterprises, were there areas of the programme where additional information or technical guidance would have been helpful?

A. ☐ yes   ☐ no   ☐ not sure; unclear

B. If "yes", please describe the specific areas.

_____

_____

Resources

13. Considering the technical advice provided to advisory groups and to enterprises, were there situations where additional information or technical guidance was needed but not available?

A. ☐ yes   ☐ no   ☐ not sure; unclear

B. If "yes", please describe the specific areas.

_____

_____

14. Is there now adequate expertise in your country to design and operate prevention programmes for small enterprises without outside assistance?

☐ yes   ☐ no   ☐ not sure

15. If "yes", is this expertise available to small businesses? (more than one alternative may be ticked)

☐ yes   ☐ no   ☐ unsure   ☐ depends on the small business owner/manager

16. Where would you go to have questions on how to prevent drug or alcohol problems in your enterprise answered?

_____

_____

Achievement and impact

17. What did you learn, positive or negative, from the project?

_____

_____

18. What was the most successful part of the project?

_____

_____

19. Does your enterprise do anything differently since the project took place? (For example, is there a different policy on the use of alcohol, are there prevention measures in the workplace, do you have contacts with other persons to discuss problems, etc.?)

_____

_____

20. For your company, did the project achieve the goals set out by the ILO and your country team?

☐ yes   ☐ no   ☐ unsure

Comment: _____

_____

21. Do you think that the enterprises involved in this project would now react differently to an employee with an alcohol or drug problem?

A. ☐ yes ☐ no ☐ not sure; not clear ☐ some yes/some no

B. If "yes" or "some yes/some no", how would reactions differ *since* the project took place?

22. In your view, is there agreement among small business owners/managers on the seriousness of alcohol or drug problems in their companies?

A. Do you think there is agreement on the seriousness of these problems?

☐ yes ☐ no ☐ not sure

B. If "yes", is the agreement that the workplaces, after the intervention programme have:

☐ improved ☐ deteriorated ☐ cannot tell/ indeterminate
☐ some think better/some think worse

C. What are the indications of any changes noticed in workplace drug and alcohol problems?

Sustainability

23. Are there government agencies, NGOs, or associations that have adopted or plan to adopt some of the practices followed in this project?

A. ☐ yes ☐ no ☐ not sure; not clear

B. If "yes", which agencies or organizations

24. How likely is it that any gains or improvements made as a result of the project will be sustained?

A. At the national level:
☐ very likely ☐ likely ☐ not sure ☐ unlikely ☐ very unlikely

B. At participating enterprises:
☐ very likely ☐ likely ☐ not sure ☐ unlikely ☐ very unlikely

25. Over what period of time are any gains likely to be sustained?

Circle a number from 1 to 10 below indicating your estimate of the length of time any gains may continue in national level agencies or organizations.

shortest time								longest time	
1	2	3	4	5	6	7	8	9	10
(several weeks)								(several years)	

Recommendations

26. If the programme to prevent drug and alcohol problems is repeated in other small businesses in your country, what changes would you recommend to increase the likelihood of its success?

Thank you!

Sample plan of action

The following plan of action is reprinted from the manual *Mobilizing small and medium businesses to prevent substance abuse*, produced by the National Drugs Agency, Ministry of Home Affairs, Malaysia, in conjunction with the ILO.

Plan of Action
Drug Abuse Prevention Programme

No.	Activities	Objectives	Target groups	Collaborating agencies	Implementation	Date/Venue	Comments
1.	Establishing the Drug Free Workplace Committee	To implement the drug prevention programme in the workplace	I. Top Management II. Human Resources III. Health and Safety IV. Workers' Union	I. National Narcotics Agency II. Company concerned	• To appoint the person to lead the committee and the coordinator to be responsible for the implementation of the project • To obtain the support and commitment (in writing) of the management • To invite the National Narcotics Agency for purposes of providing advice to the project • Form the Drug Free Workplace Committee • Establish the functions of the committee	Beginning of the programmes/ Company premises	

No.	Activities	Objectives	Target groups	Collaborating agencies	Implementation	Date/Venue	Comments
2.	**Explain the Drug Free Workplace Policy**	As a guide to all employees; explain the drug free workplace policy to the representatives	Committee members and representatives of employers	I. Drug Free Workplace Committee II. Labour Department III. Federation of Malaysian Manufacturers (FMM) IV. Malaysian Employers' Federation V. Legal Advisor VI. National Narcotics Agency	• Prepare the draft Drug Free Workplace Policy • Finalize the draft after comments from all concerned • Seek approval from top management	2 months after the formation of the committee/Company	In line with OSHA [Occupational Safety and Health Administration]
3.	**Implement the Drug Free Workplace Policy**	• Establish the Drug Free Workplace Policy • Explain the policy to all employees	All employers	I. Drug Free Workplace Committee II. National Narcotics Agency	• Circulate the Drug Free Workplace Policy to all employers • Exhibit the Drug Free Workplace Policy on notice boards Establish a procedure to ensure new employees are also informed of the policy after being recruited	2 months after the formation of the committee/Company	Briefing during monthly gatherings

No.	Activities	Objectives	Target groups	Collaborating agencies	Implementation	Date/Venue	Comments
4.	**Launching the Drug Prevention Campaign**	For promotion and publicity of drug prevention programme in the workplace	All employees and families	I. Company II. National Narcotics Agency III. Police IV. Ministry of Health V. NGOs VI. Mass media VII. Information Department	• Drug Free Workplace Committee to fix date and prepare the programme • Prepare for the launching ceremony	Immediately after explaining the policy/ Company	• Informed through Company bulletin • Optional
5.	**Implement the Drug Prevention Activities** • **Information dissemination** • **Education and enhancement of skills** • **Early intervention activities** • **Promotion of healthy alternatives (as in No. 7)** • **Involvement of the community**	Enhance the productivity, health and safety of employees and protect the workplace and families from the impact of drug abuse	All employees and families	I. Company II. National Narcotics Agency III. Police IV. Religious Department V. Health Department VI. Information Department VII. Universities	• Distribution of brochures and posters • Exhibitions • Talks • Competitions • Billboards • Bunting/Banners • In-house Training • Visits to rehabilitation centres • Health alternatives (as in No. 7)	Two activities per month throughout the year/Company premises	Committee can select activities that are suitable

No.	Activities	Objectives	Target groups	Collaborating agencies	Implementation	Date/Venue	Comments
6.	**Training of Supervisors and Employees** • **Drug Prevention** • **International Skills in Drug Prevention** • **Parenting Skills in Drug Prevention** • **Counselling Skills** • **Training the Trainers** • **Stress Management** • **Treatment and Rehabilitation**	• Enhance the knowledge and skills of employees relating to drug abuse • Enhance skills of supervisors to assist in the implementation of drug prevention/rehabilitation programmes • Create a pool of facilitators	• All employees • All supervisory staff	I. Company II. National Narcotics Agency III. Family Planning Board IV. NGOs V. Police VI. Health Department VII. Universities	• Selection of participants • Fix date, time and place of course • Prepare the materials required for the training • Prepare the training programme • Ceremony and invitation	• Company training room/hotel • Three programmes a year	Facilitators are to conduct in-house training
7.	**Promotion of health in Drug Prevention** • **Recreation** • **Family Days** • **Annual Dinners** • **Leadership Programme** • **Motivation Courses** • **Outward Bound Courses** • **Excursions** • **Talks/Forums** • **Visits to Treatment Centres**	• Create a sense of unity and teamwork among employees of the society • Encourage employees to be involved in healthy activities during their leisure time	All employees and families including members of the local community	I. Company II. National Narcotics Agency III. Ministry of Youth and Sports IV. Related Government Departments	• Select participants • Fix date, time and place • Select trainers • Prepare programme	• From time to time • Place to be selected • At least two activities per year	All employees and families are to be involved.

No.	Activities	Objectives	Target groups	Collaborating agencies	Implementation	Date/Venue	Comments
8.	**Urine Screening** • **New recruitment**	Ensure new employees are drug free	New employees	I. Company II. Staff III. Panel of doctors	• Consult panel of doctors • To identify problematic employees	• Before recruitment • As needed • Random and periodic basis	
	• **Problematic employees** • **Random screening**	To identify drug use in the workplace so that early interventions can be taken	High-risk employees All employees	I. Company II. National Narcotics Agency III. Ministry of Health IV. NGOs	• Contract National Narcotics Agency for assistance • Random screening • People who are positive should get assistance or treatment		
9.	**Involvement in Community Prevention Programmes**	To promote relationships between the company and the community	• Community • Employees • Families	I. Company II. National Narcotics Agency III. Community Leaders IV. NGOs V. Information Department	• To identify prevention programmes that are suitable for implementation • Contact the local agencies concerned and discuss their contributions towards the programme	Whatever suits the company	• Involvement should be ongoing • Optional • To be organized after all the activities from (1) to (8) have been completed

Drug Rehabilitation Programme

No.	Activities	Objectives	Target groups	Collaborating agencies	Implementation	Date/Venue	Comments
1.	Treat and rehabilitate employees that are involved with drug addiction	• Severe drug dependence behaviour among employees • To allow employees to seek treatment if they are involved • Reintegrate employees after rehabilitation	All employees	I. Company II. National Narcotics Agency III. Rehabilitation Centres	• To provide counselling services to problematic employees and families • To seek aftercare services at the National Narcotics Agency Services Centres • To obtain treatment for problematic employees • Alternative treatment modalities	Throughout the year	All concerned need to be involved.
2.	Relapse Prevention	To prevent relapse	All employees that are involved	I. Company II. National Narcotics Agency	• Urine screening • Case study • Counselling • Peer helpers' service	Throughout the year	Need the commitment of the family and community
3.	Re-entry of employees in the workplace	Restore the confidence of the employee	Employer	I. Drug Free Workplace Committee II. Employer III. National Narcotics Agency	• Counselling • Communication training • Involve the employees concerned in all programmes	During supervision of employees	Employers need to have an open mind.

Sample pages from a resource directory

The following pages are reprinted from the resource directory produced by Managing Substance Abuse in the Workplace, the South African component of the ILO pilot project, *Mobilizing Small Businesses to Prevent Substance Abuse.*

ATLANTIS ALCOHOL & DRUG CENTRE
SOCIAL WORKER
Cnr Sun & Rotterdam Str
ATLANTIS 7349

Tel No: (021) 572 7461
Fax No: (021) 572 2739

FR: 0800100083

* Assessment/Counselling/Aftercare
* Referrals
* Prevention Programmes
* Community Education/Development
* Training

TYGERBERG ALCOHOL & DRUG CENTRE
* Elsies River Service
SOCIAL WORKER
Stikland Hospital
Out Patients
STIKLAND 7530

Tel No: (021) 919 9557/8
Fax No: (021) 997 383

FR: 088001000038

* Assessment/Counselling Aftercare
* Referral
* Prevention Programmes
* Community/Education/Development
* ICS
* Training

GUGULETU/ATHLONE ALCOHOL AND DRUG CENTRE
* GUGULETU SERVICE
* ATHLONE SERVICE
SOCIAL WORKER
Saartjie Baartman Centre
Klipfontein Road
Surrey Estate
ATHLONE 7764

Tel No: (021) 638 5116
Fax No: (021) 637 5223

FR: 08S001000007 FR: 088001000014

* Assessment/Counselling/Aftercare
* Referrals
* Prevention Programmes
* Community Education
* Community Development
* ICS/Training

MITCHELLS PLAIN ALCOHOL AND DRUG CENTRE
SOCIAL WORKER
11 Daphne Crescent
Eastridge
MITCHELLS PLAIN 7785

PO Box 761
MITCHELLS PLAIN

Tel No: 397 4617/2196
Fax No: 397 4617

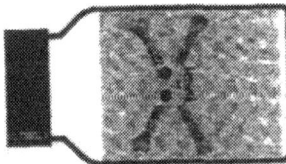

FR: 08001000090

* Assessment/Counselling/ Aftercare
* Referrals
* Prevention Programmes
* Community Education/Development
* Training

Satellite Offices: * Cape Town * Milnerton * Kensington * Khayelitsha

AFFILIATED BODIES

Cape Town Drug Counselling Centre
PR: 9015175
DIRECTOR
MRS CATHY KARASSELLOS
1 Roman Road
OBSERVATORY 7925

PO Box 56
OBSERVATORY 7935

Tel No: (021) 447 8026
Fax No: (021) 447 8818
Email: ctdcct@iafrica-com

FR: 088001000076

SERVICES OFFERED
* Assessment/Consultation
* School Prevention Programmes
* Referral
* Out-patient Treatment
* Community Education
* Training
* Aftercare

**SANCA: NORTHERN CAPE
ALCOHOL AND DRUG CENTRE**

FR: 100000860009

SENIOR SOCIAL WORKER
MRS SUSANNE VAN TONDER
18 Market Square
KIMBERLEY 8301

PO Box 909
KIMBERLEY 8300

Tel No: (053) 831 1699
Fax No: (053) 832 5216

SERVICES OFFERED
* Assessment
* Referral
* Consultation
* Counselling
* Community Education

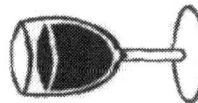

**SANCA: SANPARK
COMMUNITY SUPPORT**

FR: 055000120007
PR: 9005994

DIRECTOR
DR HENNIE JOUBERT
94 Park Street
KLERKSDORP 2570

PO Box 491
KLERKSDORP 2570

Tel No: (018) 464 2008
Fax No: (018) 464 2581
Cell No: 083 673 0245

DEDICATED PROGRAMMES

PROVINCIAL REPRESENTATIVE

Email: psycure@lantic.co.za

Helderberg Against Dependence
HEAD OF SERVICE
Dummer Street
SOMERSET WEST 7130
Tel No: (021) 852 4820

* Counselling
* Community Education

George Alcohol & Drug Centre
HEAD OF SERVICE
MS YVETTE DU PLESSIS
Room 4
Tommy Joubert Building (North)
Courteney Street
ROSEMOOR 6530

PO Box 2310
GEORGE 6530
Tel/Fax No: (044) 884 0674

* Counselling
* Community Education
* ICS

Knysna Alcohol & Drug Centre
HEAD OF SERVICE
MS LYNN ALLEN
Grey Street
KNYSNA

PO Box 1290
KNYSNA 6570
Tel/Fax No: (044) 382 5260

* Counselling
* Community Education

Mosselbay Alcohol & Drug Centre
Amalgamated with FAMSA
Tel/Fax No: (044) 691 1411

Sample policy statements

The key elements of a substance abuse policy reproduced in the *Manual on prevention of substance abuse in small enterprises*, produced by the Federation of Indian Chambers of Commerce and Industry (FICCI) Socio-Economic Development Foundation (India) in conjunction with the ILO.

As a first step towards institutionalizing the [substance abuse prevention] programme, an enterprise must have a meticulously worded policy on alcohol and drugs. Such a policy should be evolved by management in close consultation with workers and their representatives, so as to have a consensus on:

- measures to prohibit or restrict the availability of the substances of abuse in the workplace;
- measures to reduce alcohol- and drug-related problems through informational, educational and training programmes;
- prevention of substance abuse in the workplace through informational, educational and training programmes;
- identification, assistance and referral of those with alcohol- and drug-related problems in the workplace;
- care, treatment and rehabilitation of those with alcohol- and drug-related problems in the workplace;
- code of conduct and grievance redressal and disciplinary system for substance abuse prevention;
- non-discrimination in employment of persons with post or current alcohol- or drug-related problems.

A sample policy taken from *Mobilizing small and medium businesses to prevent substance abuse*, produced by the National Drugs Agency, Ministry of Home Affairs, Malaysia, and the ILO.

(Name of company) is committed to providing a safe work environment in accordance with OSHA (1994) and to foster the well-being and health of its employees. That commitment is jeopardized when any (name of company) employee uses *dadah* [the Malaysian word for illicit drugs] on the job, comes to work with these substances present in his/her body or possesses, distributes or sells *dadah* in the workplace. (Name of company) has established the following policy with regard to *dadah* to ensure that we can meet our obligations to our employees, shareholders, customers and the public.

The good of this policy is to balance our respect for individuals with the need to maintain a safe, productive and *dadah*-free environment. The intent of this policy is to offer a helping hand to those who need it, while sending a clear message that *dadah* use is incompatible with working at (name of company).

1. It is a violation for any employee to possess, distribute or sell *dadah* in the workplace in accordance with DDA 1952 and OSHA 1994.

2. It is a violation for any employee to report to work under the influence of *dadah*.

3. It is the company's policy to plan and implement primary prevention programmes relating to *dadah* for employees and their families.

4. It is the company's policy to provide referral services to assist employees that are involved or have a *dadah* problem.

5. The company will test all employees at pre-employment or whenever the company has reasonable suspicion that an employee has used *dadah* during working or non-working hours, on or off the company's premises.

6. It is the policy of the company to commit the resources necessary to achieve and maintain a *dadah*-free work environment.

7. Violation of any aspect of this policy may result in severe disciplinary action at the company's discretion.

Self-assessment tools

How can I tell if I have a problem with drugs or alcohol?

Drug and alcohol problems can affect every one of us, regardless of age, sex, race, marital status, place of residence, income level, or lifestyle.

You may have a problem with drugs or alcohol if:

- You can't predict whether or not you will use drugs or get drunk.

- You believe that in order to have fun you need to drink and/or use drugs.

- You turn to alcohol and/or drugs after a confrontation or argument, or to relieve uncomfortable feelings.

- You drink more or use more drugs to get the same effect that you previously got with smaller amounts.

- You drink and/or use drugs alone.

- You remember how last night began, but not how it ended, so you're worried you may have a problem.

- You have trouble at work or in school because of your drinking or drug use.

- You make promises to yourself or others that you'll stop getting drunk or using drugs.

- You feel alone, scared, miserable and depressed.

The CAGE questionnaire

The CAGE questionnaire was developed for the early detection of problem drinkers. It consists of only four questions which yield a positive predictive value of over 80 per cent in the description of problem drinkers and self-referred alcoholics in treatment centres. In the workplace situation it obviously does not have the same high predictive value and would be of little use as a screening instrument. Nevertheless, it could still be useful as a case finding instrument in high-risk groups.

The most positive aspect of the CAGE instrument is its simplicity and low cost. Two or more affirmative answers to its four questions are sufficient to identify 80 per cent of the problem drinkers in a high-risk population. The name CAGE is an acronym formed from the initial of the key word in each question. The questions are as follows:

1. Have you ever felt that you should **C**ut down on your drinking?

2. Have people **A**nnoyed you by criticizing your drinking?

3. Have you ever felt bad or **G**uilty about your drinking?

4. Have you ever had a drink first thing in the morning to steady your nerves or get rid of a hangover (**E**ye-opener)?

The MAST questionnaire

The Michigan Alcoholism Screening Test (MAST) questionnaire is one of the most widely used tests in the identification or description of problem drinkers in western societies. There exists a short version, called the Brief MAST Questionnaire, which consists of ten questions for self-assessment or interview. The questionnaire is intended for secondary prevention efforts, targeted at groups or individuals who have already been identified as being at risk. The answers to the questions are either "yes" or "no", but the values attributed to the responses vary from 0 to 5. The values are indicated after each possible response and a total score of more than five indicates problem drinking. The questions are as follows:

Circle the correct answer

1. Do you feel you are a normal drinker?   Yes (0)   No (2)

2. Do friends or relatives think you are a normal drinker?   Yes (0)   No (2)

3. Have you ever attended a meeting of Alcoholics Anonymous (AA)?   Yes (5)   No (0)

4. Have you ever lost friends or girlfriends/boyfriends because of drinking?   Yes (2)   No (0)

5. Have you ever got into trouble at work because of drinking?   Yes (2)   No (0)

6. Have you ever neglected your obligations to your family or your work
   for two or more days in a row because you were drinking?   Yes (2)   No (0)

7. Have you ever had delirium tremens (DTs), severe shaking, heard
   voices, or seen things that weren't there after heavy drinking?   Yes (2)   No (0)

8. Have you ever gone to anyone for help about your drinking?   Yes (5)   No (0)

9. Have you ever been in hospital because of drinking?   Yes (5)   No (0)

10. Have you ever been arrested for drunk driving or driving after drinking?   Yes (2)   No (0)

The WHO alcohol use disorder identification test-AUDIT

In 1987 a WHO study developed a valuable instrument for assessing alcohol-related problems on a triple scale: social damage; physical injury; and degree of dependency. The instrument is known as the AUDIT, and it seems to be the most promising self-assessment test available for secondary prevention in the context of early identification.

AUDIT is a ten-item self-assessment which can lead people from ignorance of their problem through contemplation to action. It should be made available to all at-risk personnel and to those individuals who are suspected of being problem drinkers. Re-testing at three-month intervals can give positive feedback if scores improve. The only danger is that drinkers who score in the caution zone may consider that this means that they do not have a problem, which is yet another manifestation of the prevention paradox.

The AUDIT Questionnaire

Circle the number that comes closest to the patient's answer.

1. How often do you have a drink containing alcohol?				
(0) Never	(1) Monthly or less	(2) 2 to 4 times a week	(3) 2 to 3 times a week	(4) 4 or more times a week

2. How many drinks containing alcohol do you have on a typical day when you are drinking? *				
(0) 1 or 2	(1) 3 or 4	(2) 5 or 6	(3) 7 to 9	(4) 10 or more

3. How often do you have six or more drinks on one occasion?				
(0) Never	(1) Less than monthly	(2) Monthly	(3) Weekly	(4) Daily or almost daily

4. How often during the last year have you found that you were not able to stop drinking once you had started?				
(0) Never	(1) Less than monthly	(2) Monthly	(3) Weekly	(4) Daily or almost daily

5. How often during the last year have you failed to do what was normally expected from you because of drinking?				
(0) Never	(1) Less than monthly	(2) Monthly	(3) Weekly	(4) Daily or almost daily

6. How often during the last year have you needed a first drink in the morning to get yourself going after a heavy drinking session?				
(0) Never	(1) Less than monthly	(2) Monthly	(3) Weekly	(4) Daily or almost daily

7. How often during the last year have you had a feeling of guilt or remorse after drinking?				
(0) Never	(1) Less than monthly	(2) Monthly	(3) Weekly	(4) Daily or almost daily

8. How often during the last year have you been unable to remember what happened the night before because you had been drinking?				
(0) Never	(1) Less than monthly	(2) Monthly	(3) Weekly	(4) Daily or almost daily

9. Have you or someone else been injured as a result of your drinking?		
(0) No	(2) Yes, but not in the last year	(4) Yes, during the last year

10. Has a relative, friend, doctor, or other health worker been concerned about your drinking or suggested you cut down?		
(0) No	(2) Yes, but not in the last year	(4) Yes, during the last year

* In determining the response categories, it has been assumed that one "drink" contains 10 grams of alcohol. In countries where the alcohol content of a standard drink differs by more than 25 per cent from 10 grams, the response should be modified accordingly.

Record the sum of individual item scores here. _____

N.B. • A score of less than 11 points: no danger
  • Between 11 and 15: Caution – watch out
  • Over 15: You have a problem – seek assistance.

www.ingramcontent.com/pod-product-compliance
Lightning Source LLC
Chambersburg PA
CBHW080841270326
41927CB00013B/3063